The Buildings of Salisbury

RICHARD K. MORRISS

With photographs by Ken Hoverd

ALAN SUTTON PUBLISHING LIMITED

First published in the United Kingdom in 1994
Alan Sutton Publishing Limited
Phoenix Mill · Far Thrupp · Stroud · Gloucestershire

First published in the United States of America in 1994
Alan Sutton Publishing Inc. · 83 Washington Street · Dover
NH 03820

British Library Cataloguing-in-Publication Data

ISBN 0–7509–0563–8

A catalogue record for this book is available from the British
Library

Library of Congress Cataloging-in-Publication Data applied
for

Cover illustrations: front: St George's House just outside the
North Gate; *front inset*: The fourteenth century North Gate of
Cathedral Close; *back:* the west front of the cathedral.

Typeset in 11/14 Times.
Typesetting and origination by
Alan Sutton Publishing Limited.
Printed in Great Britain by
Ebenezer Baylis, Worcester.

The Buildings of Salisbury

Ray.

As Cookery books are probably not of much interest — this little memento of Salisbury might be more appropriate!

Martin

June 1998.

2 The Interior of Salisbury Cathedral

Contents

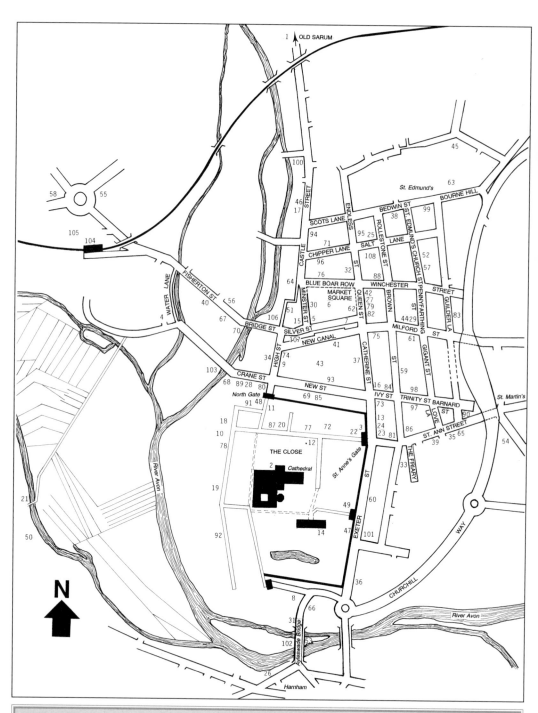

Salisbury. The numbers on the map refer to building numbers in the captions.

Introduction

The town of New Saresbyri with the suburbes of Harnham
Bridge and Fischertown is t[w]o good miles in cumpance . . .
Ther be many fair streates in the cite . . . and especially the
High Streate, and the Castel Streate, so caullid bycause it lyeth
as a way to the castelle of Old-Saresbyry.

(John Leland *c*.1540)

New Salisbury is one of the world's finest medieval cities and
one of its major tourist destinations. The city still retains most
of its original layout and boasts an exceptionally fine
collection of historic buildings dating from the medieval period
onwards – all dominated by the tallest spire in England. So rich
is Salisbury's architectural legacy that it was chosen as one of
the all too few cities to be surveyed in detail by the Royal
Commission on Historic Monuments – and to date their
excellent work has resulted in one voluminous volume on the
city, another on the Close and one on the cathedral – with
others on that medieval masterpiece planned in due course.
Excluding the cathedral itself, nearly 700 buildings proved
worthy of the Commission's attention – and their remit was
only to study buildings built before 1850. Salisbury is not a
particularly large city – with a population of less than 40,000 –
and the survival rate of its historic buildings is exceptional.

A mile or so to the north the brooding hillfort site of Old
Sarum overlooks the city down below in the river meadows. It
is deserted now, a place of ghosts and legend. Yet this is where
medieval Salisbury used to be, and the interwoven tales of the
three main settlements in this area – the third being Wilton, a
few miles to the west – provides an object lesson in the ebb
and flow of urban fortunes.

People have lived in this part of England for thousands of
years and less than 10 miles to the north-west of Salisbury is

prehistoric Britain's most famous monument – Stonehenge. The hillfort at Old Sarum was probably occupied some time before the Roman conquest, in the Iron Age, and would have been a regional centre for the local tribe and a place of refuge in time of war. The natural defences of the hill top were reinforced by scarping the slopes and ringing the central area with two banks separated by a deep ditch. These earthworks enclosed an area of just under 30 acres, and the time and effort needed to carry out this work show just how sophisticated the social structure of the local tribe must have been.

The Romans do not seem to have occupied the fort itself, but did make use of it as a survey point in their massive road building programme. A settlement developed along their new road just to the west of the fort in what is now the village of Stratford-sub-Castle. The name Stratford, incidentally, is Saxon, and means the place where the Roman road, or 'street', crossed the river by a ford. Stratford-upon-Avon's name has the same origins – and both fords crossed a River Avon, though not the same one. Very little is known about the Roman settlement of Sorviodunum but it must have been an important route centre in its day, being the point where roads from Cirencester (Corinium), Winchester (Venta Belgarum) and Bath (Aqua Sulis) met the main highway from London to Dorchester (Durnovaria) and the south-west. The settlement no doubt declined after the Roman legions departed, but the *Anglo-Saxon Chronicle* recorded that a great battle was fought at 'Searobyrg' in around AD 552 at which the invading West Saxons beat the British; this is considered to have been at or near Old Sarum.

What happened to Old Sarum and the former Roman town in the next four hundred years or so is unknown, but it may have continued to be some type of administrative centre for the immediate area for a time. Possibly as early as the seventh century there was some settlement at Wilton, down in the well-wooded and well-watered valley 2 miles or so to the west. This developed into the new regional centre fairly quickly, becoming a provincial capital of the kingdom of Wessex; the Saxon 'scire' of Wiltshire was named after it. It did not, however, have a good defensive site – as King Alfred discovered in 871 when he was defeated there by the Danes. Possibly as a direct result of that reverse, Alfred refortified Old Sarum to act as a refuge for the people of Wilton in times

A Victorian engraving of
New Salisbury, with the
inevitable backdrop of
the cathedral's spire. The
close link between the
city and the agriculture
of the region has also
been a continual factor in
its prosperity.

of war. Following another Danish raid on Wilton in 1003 it
seems that some people began to move from there to Old
Sarum on a more permanent basis – including the moneyers.
The old hillfort thus became the focus of a small Saxon
settlement, but Wilton continued to be the main administrative
centre.

After the Norman conquest, the new order controlled their
new subjects by the use of the castle. The hillfort at Old Sarum
was an obvious site for one, and a simple 'motte-and-bailey'
had been built by 1069. Six years later, at the Council of
London, the Normans reorganized the religious affairs of the
country. One of the changes meant that any cathedral sited in a
village had to be replaced by one in a larger centre of
population. The united diocese of Sherbourne and Ramsbury
were ordered to have a new cathedral in the fortress town of
Old Sarum – by this time being referred to as 'Sarisberie'. The

later shortened version – Sarum – is thought to have been a misreading of the real name; by the early thirteenth century an 'l' had replaced the 'r' in the full name. The combination of castle and cathedral led to the growth of the Norman town, though most of its people actually lived in suburbs outside its eastern gate. There was simply very little room to spare within the prehistoric defences.

It was the cramped nature of the site that eventually led to its decline, particularly because of conflict between castle and cathedral. The clergy claimed that on the water-starved hill they were forced to buy water from the military, that the soldiers often abused the priests and refused pilgrims entry, and that their accommodation was far too limited. Amongst other complaints were the harshness of the sun reflecting off the chalk hillside, and the cold that caused rheumatism! By the end of the twelfth century they had reached breaking point.

1 The Norman castle built within the ramparts of Old Sarum continued in use as an administrative centre and fortress for a century or so after the creation of the new city in the valley below, but was virtually derelict by the end of the fourteenth century.

Bishop Herbert Poore can be credited with the idea of moving the cathedral to a new site and obtained royal permission from Richard I. It was clear from the start that the move would not only entail just the cathedral itself – but would result in the creation of a completely new town to serve it. By the early thirteenth century, outline planning was well under way but the move was only started after the end of the calamitous reign of King John, by which time Herbert's brother, Richard, was bishop. The final go-ahead was given by Pope Honorius III in 1219.

Wilton would have been the logical place to have moved the cathedral to, but instead a completely new site was chosen. One lovely medieval story relates how the bishop, just anxious to get out of the confines of Old Sarum, vowed to build his new church wherever an arrow fired from the city's ramparts would land. The arrow hit a deer, and the wounded beast ran down into the water

1 In the early years of this century the footings of St Osmund's eleventh-century cathedral at Old Sarum were exposed, tidied and left in view. Even though only a masonry ground plan remains, it has enough information to tell us a great deal about the complicated development of this great church in its comparatively short life.

2 Salisbury Cathedral is one of the great Gothic masterpieces of the world, and the purest example of the Early English form. The spire that dominates the city is, at 404 ft high, the tallest in Britain. It was not part of the original design, but added so sympathetically it is difficult to see how else the great church could have otherwise been finished.

3 From the very start, the Close and the city were kept apart. This is a view of St Ann's Gate in the early 1900s. One of the signs on the wall behind the lamp-post is directed towards motor cars – when drivers had time to get out and read the small print!

meadows by the Avon before collapsing – and the site was thus chosen. It is not known what happened to the deer! The real reasons for the new site were, alas, more pragmatic. The area chosen was on level and well-drained meadows, with the Avon on the west and south sides and the slope of Milford Hill to the east. It was close to three small existing settlements – Fisherton to the west, East Harnham to the south and St Martin's. All this land was owned by the church already, and there was plenty of the two commodities so lacking on the hill top – water and space. Planned new towns were not rare in the medieval period. Indeed, they were fairly common. Few, however, succeeded, and Salisbury was one of the most successful.

A temporary wooden chapel was erected in 1219, and the grand stone-laying ceremony for the new cathedral was planned for 28 April 1220 – St Vital the Martyr's Day. Bishop Poore went to great expense to lay on a grand feast for his

4 One of the natural advantages of the site of New Salisbury was its abundant water supply. The Avon was easy to harness, and many other leats were taken off it. This one fed mills in Fisherton; the road alongside is Water Lane.

invited guests, who included Henry III and the Archbishop of Canterbury. Unfortunately, the king and most of the important guests became involved in negotiations with the Welsh at Shrewsbury and did not attend. Most of the assembled throng at the ceremony were ordinary folk from Old Sarum and the surrounding villages.

Work on the cathedral went well and during the early 1220s the clergy began to move into their new houses around its spacious Close. To the north and east of the Close the New Salisbury took shape and was given added impetus by a charter of Henry III in 1227 that allowed it a market, fairs and defences. The new city's streets were laid out in a fairly regular grid pattern, creating 'islands' (or 'insulae') between them that later became called 'chequers'. Gradually more and more people were encouraged to live in New Salisbury, tempted by generous 'burgage' plots and the profitable possibilities of

5 The predecessors of the present fifteenth-century Poultry Cross stood in the south-western corner of the market place. Now there are infill buildings between it and the smaller surviving open space.

trading at the market and enjoying other urban privileges away from the restrictions of the old city. The sheer size of the present market place in the centre of the city is often cause for comment – and originally it was even larger. The success of the market was crucial for the success of the city. It attracted traders and merchants to the city and their rents, along with market tolls, helped pay for the new cathedral rising in its spacious close.

The success of the market also led to the decline of both Old Sarum and Wilton. The military continued to maintain the castle at Old Sarum, but most of its townsfolk quickly resettled in the new city below. The county gaol and sheriff both remained there until the start of the fourteenth century – but by the end of that century the castle was derelict. Writing in the early sixteenth century, John Leland recorded that 'There hath beene houses in tyme of mynd inhabited in the est suburbe of

6 Salisbury's market place is still one of the larger ones in the country. This view is towards the southern side, where all the buildings have encroached into what was once an even larger open area.

Old Saresbyri, but [now] ther is not one house nother in Old-Saresbyri or without'. Old Sarum is still remembered as the most rotten of rotten boroughs. Until the early nineteenth century this deserted ghost town still sent two members to parliament – one of them being William Pitt the Elder. In 1826 the radical MP and author William Cobbett wrote 'It was impossible to stand on this accursed spot, without swelling with indignation against the base and plundering and murderous sons of corruption'. Six years later the Reform Act finally abolished the rotten boroughs for good.

Wilton's decline was more gradual and less dramatic. As well as taking away much of the older town's market trade, New Salisbury also became the main route centre of the area – especially after the construction of Ayleswade Bridge across the Avon by Bishop Bingham in about 1240. This diverted one of the principal routes away from Wilton and thus took away much of

7 A general view down Butcher Row and Fish Street, showing the rich texture of Salisbury's streetscapes. It also shows how it is possible to build new facades that fit in with their ancient neighbours.

the older town's trade. By the end of the thirteenth century New Salisbury had overtaken Wilton in both population and prosperity.

Cathedral and commerce gave the new city its initial impetus, but the latter part of the thirteenth century also saw the development of another important factor in its growth – the wool trade. Surrounded by good sheep-rearing land New Salisbury naturally became the main centre of the local industry, initially dealing in the export of raw wool. During the course of the fourteenth century, England began to turn to producing woollen cloth rather than simply exporting fleeces. Well supplied with running water to power the fulling mills used in the treatment of the cloth, Salisbury had, by the end of the century, become one of the major textile-producing towns in the country. Throughout the following centuries, many of its more important residents were involved in the woollen industry, and several of their grand houses still survive.

8 Briefly, Salisbury threatened the universities of Oxford and Cambridge. Unsettled students from Oxford were taught at the de Vaux College in the 1260s, but the venture failed. Traces of the college buildings – notably the right-hand corner masonry – survive in the later buildings bearing the name.

9 Arriving in Salisbury in the summer of 1668 Samuel Pepys wrote 'Come to the George Inne, where lay in a silk bed; and a very good diet'. Next day he complained bitterly as he 'paid the reckoning, which was so exorbitant'. When he stayed, the fourteenth-century framing facing High Street was covered with pargetted plaster. The once busy courtyard of this important inn survived more or less intact until 1967, when the present rather utilitarian shopping centre was built in its stead.

The city was also patronized by the court, as the royal hunting retreat of Clarendon was only a few miles away. For a short while, there was even a chance that Salisbury would become a new Oxford or Cambridge. Displaced students from Oxford were offered accommodation in De Vaux college, just south of the Close, in the 1260s, but it failed to develop. Nevertheless, by the end of the fourteenth century Salisbury, with a population of around 5,000, was one of the ten largest towns in England and remained so for two centuries.

For all this time the city was, ultimately, controlled by the bishop. His guild hall stood in the market place as a symbol of his authority. The growing wealth of the townsfolk led to demands for more independence to run their own affairs but time and time again these were refused, leading to simmering rancour and considerable tension. The early decision by Bishop

Poore to separate his Close from his city was seen as a wise move, and the construction of the Close wall in the mid-fourteenth century a pragmatic one. Even after the Church had lost much of its power during the Reformation, the bishop retained his control over Salisbury, and it was only in 1612 that James I granted its citizens their autonomy.

By this time, the city was suffering from over fifty years of economic stagnation. The wool trade had declined as Salisbury's monopoly on it was broken, and the innate conservatism of an industry that had been so dominant for centuries made it slow to react to change. In the early seventeenth century the town was hard hit by plague on several occasions, the worst occurring in 1627 when close on 400 died from it. The partly abandoned city was virtually given over to anarchy and only really saved by its radical mayor, John Ivie.

10 The early eighteenth-century ashlar elegance of Arundells, in the Close, is literally skin deep. The frontage block is essentially a century older, and in turn hides the surviving parts of a thirteenth-century cross-wing to a vanished hall. This was one of the houses of the early canons of the new cathedral.

Many of the economic ills suffered by manufacturing towns like Salisbury were inevitably blamed on the king, and when the Civil War broke out the city was strongly in favour of Parliament. Being undefended, however, it was not of any great strategic importance to either side and could easily be by-passed anyway. Nevertheless, it was briefly occupied by Prince Maurice and a Royalist force in 1642, and by Edmund Ludlow's Parliamentary forces in 1644. Later that year, King Charles himself entered Salisbury with the main army and left a small garrison behind. These took up quarters in the Close but were taken by the returning Parliamentary troops, who were, in turn, forced to flee in January 1645. In the Commonwealth that followed Cromwell's final victory, Salisbury suffered. Its economic decline continued and religious persecution was accompanied by a virtual breakdown in the civil administration. The cathedral and its Close were

11 Bishop Seth Ward's Matrons' College, just inside the North Gate of the Close, symbolizes the prosperity of the Restoration period in Salisbury. It was designed to house ten clergy widows and opened in 1682. The symmetry of the red brick and stone decorated design, with its central pediment, has led to the assumption that it was by Ward's friend, Sir Christopher Wren – but there is no proof of this.

violated by religious zealots. The Restoration could not have come too soon.

After 1660 Salisbury revived, a fact shown by its many fine late seventeenth- and very early eighteenth-century buildings. The diarist Samuel Pepys, a friend of the remarkable bishop, Seth Ward, in an odd back-handed compliment wrote of Salisbury as 'a very brave place . . . The city great, I think greater than Hereford'. It became something of a fashionable focus for the local gentry and an important centre of the rapidly improving road network – its inns and hotels providing a welcome break for weary travellers. Writing in the 1730s, Defoe commented that 'Salisbury itself is indeed a large and pleasant city; . . . The people of Salisbury are gay and rich, and have a flourishing trade; and there is a great deal of good manners and good company among them; I mean, among the citizens, beside what is found among the gentlemen. . . .'. He

12 The peace and tranquillity of Salisbury's Close in the early years of this century captured on this postcard may today occasionally be interrupted by the thousands of visitors to it – but it is still a relaxing place to be. Little has changed – apart from the removal of the ivy from the houses.

13 The rich diversity of Salisbury's buildings can be seen in this view of just part of White Hart Chequer, fronting St John's Street. The twin-gabled portion on the right dates to the sixteenth century and is of rendered timber-framing. The taller central portion, with its fairly thin timbers, dates to the mid seventeenth century. At the far left, the upper floor was a grand dining room added in the early nineteenth century on to the top of an earlier structure.

14 The Bishop's Palace retains some elements of Bishop Poore's original home of the 1220s – notably the vaulted undercroft of the solar once attached to the great hall. It has been altered many times since, especially in the fifteenth and seventeenth centuries, and thus provides a remarkably complex story for anyone wishing to unravel it. It is now part of the Cathedral School.

was not so impressed with the unique water channels that had ran down all the main roads since the city was laid out. These may once have been a useful source of clean water but by the eighteenth century they were 'always dirty, full of wet and filth and weeds, even in the middle of summer'. They were finally done away with in the nineteenth century.

By the time Victoria came to the throne, the hoped for industrial growth of the cloth and carpet trade that was to have resulted from the opening of a new canal to the sea had failed to develop. The late arrival of the railways did make the city an important railway junction and the old village of Fisherton grew rapidly as a result. By then the manufacture of woollen goods had disappeared and Salisbury relied mainly on its role as a regional market centre. By 1861 its population had grown to around 14,000 and it continued to rise steadily but not dramatically. Salisbury remained the archetypal sleepy cathedral city, the Melchester of Thomas Hardy and, combined with its sister city of Winchester, Trollope's Barchester. In many ways it has changed little since then. Now it has a population of less than 40,000, is still a regional centre for shopping and marketing, and one of the most attractive cities in Europe.

Architectural Character

With its grid pattern of wide streets laid out on a level greenfield site, New Salisbury has, in some ways, more in common with a mid-western American town than it has with most other English medieval cities. In many streets it is possible to see from one end of the city to the other, and Salisbury certainly has none of the narrow winding lanes of York or the mysterious back alleys of Shrewsbury. Many other planned medieval towns were divided up into rectangular plots, or 'insulae', but usually the buildings faced on to a principal street and their long burgage plots backed on to a narrow service lane shared by the houses on the next main street across. In Salisbury, there were no such back lanes through the chequers – leaving only spacious streets even on the edges of the new development. Again, unlike in those other towns, it was the chequers themselves that became important in the identification of properties rather than the streets. The chequers were, and are, all named, either after an inn or a house or sometimes an individual.

Few cities have retained so much of a planned medieval layout in such entirety – although there have been one or two changes. The great market place once extended as far south as New Canal and further west than St Thomas's church. Within a few decades, the temporary stalls within it became less and less temporary, and were eventually replaced by permanent buildings – the Butcher's and Oatmeal Rows, for example, and the series of buildings now hemming in St Thomas's churchyard. This process of 'market infilling' was quite a

common one and usually went much further than it has done at Salisbury.

The undoubted delights of Salisbury's streetscapes rely heavily on the buildings themselves, and few cities can boast so varied, yet ultimately so harmonious, a collection. Apart from the obvious historical importance of these buildings, the very texture of Salisbury is a constant source of delectation – a rich mix of timber-framing, flint, ashlar, brick, tile-hanging and slate.

Ever since it started, New Salisbury has been rigidly divided into two parts – the religious enclave around the cathedral, and the secular world outside. Since the early fourteenth century that division has been enforced by the defensive Close wall. Although many of those now living in the Close, surely one of the most prestigious addresses in England, no longer have any direct link with the church, its tranquillity is still a world apart

15 In most towns such a set of historic buildings, on Minster Street, would be picked out in all the tourist guides as being something special. Indeed, they are special – but Salisbury has literally hundreds of special buildings and it is possible to get rather blasé about them. The corner building and the Haunch of Venison are both of mid fifteenth century date, the twin-gabled house to the right only slightly later and once one large dwelling.

from the busy city without. In the early eighteenth century, Defoe considered that 'the Circle of Ground wall'd in adjacent to the Cathedral . . . [was] . . . like another City'. In the early days, the separation between the two was more obvious in the architecture as well and in some respects still is. The wealthy canons in the Close were granted huge plots in which to build their houses. The townsfolk, although generously provided for by the standard of other medieval cities, lived in humbler dwellings on smaller plots. As the merchants and traders got gradually wealthier, the architectural distinctions gradually diminished.

At the start of the thirteenth century, most houses in the city would have been built of timber-framing, but the canons were ordered to build their new houses in the Close in stone. Stone was an expensive material in medieval England and one generally confined to the most prestigious buildings – churches

16 Despite the generous proportions of burgage plots in Salisbury's chequers, properties were sub-divided and, as in many other medieval towns, houses tended to become elongated. Everyone wanted a street frontage, so in order to fit every one in, narrow houses developed. This example in Ivy Street, on the now partly depopulated Antelope Chequer, shows a typical frontage block with narrow extensions to the rear.

17 There are only occasional narrow back alleys in New Salisbury, because of the city's chequer pattern. This one, Ivy Place, is just off Castle Street. The terrace on the right is of late eighteenth-century date, built of brick covered with render. The doves in the foreground are real!

18 The Wardrobe, 58 The Close, despite being radically altered over the years, retains the thirteenth-century masonry carcass of a classic 'H-shaped' hall house. The central open hall was flanked by two-storey cross-wings at either end – the solar block to the right, the services to the left. The house was substantially remodelled in the late sixteenth century and the main front 'tidied' in the early nineteenth century. It is now a military museum.

and castles in particular. Salisbury has no good building stone of its own and the cathedral itself was built of limestone quarried 12 miles away at Chilmark, where stone-working continued until just before the Second World War. The distance from the city to those quarries simply added to the expense at a time when transport was primitive and time-consuming.

Chilmark limestone could be cut easily and worked into smoothly faced regular blocks that could be laid in regular courses – ashlared – but only a handful of secular buildings were built entirely of it. Amongst these are Church House on Crane Street and the house of John Hall on New Canal, both built in the late fifteenth century. Usually the stone was only used for decoration and to help bind together a much cheaper form of masonry – flint. Only in England has flint been used so extensively for construction purposes. In their natural state flints are small pieces of very hard silica, usually black,

19 This fireplace and the decorated plaster frieze and ceiling that go with it, were part of a late sixteenth-century extension to the King's House on the west side of the Close.

Flint walling in its most primitive form, roughly knapped and laid in heavy mortar as rubble.

Properly knapped and well-laid flint in even courses and with thinner mortar.

A typical hybrid construction of knapped flint and ashlar blocks, forming an attractive chequer pattern.

A nineteenth-century version of flint walling, with the knapped flints alternating with brick courses.

The only local building stone came in sizes little larger than pebbles – flint. It needed quite thick layers of mortar and often other types of building material were used with it to provide additional strength.

20 The peculiarly named Aula le Stage, 21 The Close, is built of knapped flint. It is one of the most complex buildings in the city but its secrets have been unravelled by the Royal Commission. The front owes much to a very sympathetic remodelling in the early eighteenth-century when the right hand gable and porch were added to match the left-hand gable - that had, in turn, been remodelled two centuries previously. The bulk of the house was built in the thirteenth century and altered in the fourteenth, fifteenth and sixteenth centuries.

usually rounded, and often simply picked up from ploughed fields. They were the product of glaciation, often being carried for many miles away from their natural bedrock by the glaciers. When used for building they were carefully placed in courses and held together by thick mortar. The flints on the outer faces were often split, or knapped, and as a result had flat surfaces that were designed to improve their appearance and colour. Often, the flint walls would be rendered anyway. Where more structural strength was needed, around windows and at the corners for example, better quality stone was used – in Salisbury, usually from Chilmark. Later in the medieval period and after, interesting chequer patterns were sometimes developed with squares of knapped flint alternating with squares of ashlared stone or brick. Typical examples are parts of the Bishop's Palace and Harnham Mill.

Knapped flint has a feeling of antiquity about it, even if the

buildings are relatively new. Generally, the earlier the building the less tidy the coursing of the flints – such as in the early thirteenth-century chancel of St Martin's. Later the flints could become almost regimented in their coursing, as in Pugin's mid-nineteenth-century St Osmund's. The original canonical houses around the Close were probably built of flint, but the material was used sparingly outside in the city where timber-frames once dominated.

Over centuries, timber-framed buildings developed from primitive structures into sophisticated pieces of architectural engineering. Usually, felled trees were worked in the carpenter's yard, where they were sawn, shaped and then slotted together into the individual frames required on the yard floor. Individual joints were marked by Roman numerals gouged into the face of the wood. Then the frames were dismantled and the timbers taken to site and re-erected. The 'panels' between the timbers

21 Flint and ashlar chequer walling is seen at its best in the ground floor of Harnham Mill, built in about 1500. The upper portion is of much later brickwork.

22 Good ashlar masonry was fairly rare in Salisbury, but several of the larger houses around the Close were refaced in the material in the eighteenth century. This is the elegant west front of Malmesbury House, built in the early years of the eighteenth century by James Harris using stone from the Close wall.

23 This ashlar-faced shop with living quarters above, on St John Street, was built in the early nineteenth century. It fronted the workshops of stone mason William Osmond, who may well have designed and built it. The neoclassical style is influenced by the Greek Revival – slightly ironic in view of the fact that Osmond was one of the masons used by that great propagandist of the Gothic, Augustus Pugin.

obviously had to be filled in once the timber skeleton of the building was ready. In Salisbury there is evidence that many of the earliest timber-framed buildings had chalk rubble infill, which may account for the heavy timbers and the use of diagonals and braces in the frames. Later, the infills were usually of 'wattle-and-daub' – a mix of dung and clay daubed on to a fixed frame of wattles interwoven between vertical staves that was then covered with a plaster skin.

Medieval panels tended to be quite large, and had to be braced. The bracing patterns in Salisbury are both architecturally fascinating and aesthetically pleasing – including St Andrew's crosses and curves both concave and convex. The size of panels gradually decreased towards the late sixteenth century. An alternate style to rectangular framing was close-studding, in which vertical 'studs' were placed close together in the frame. Timber-frames were also often jettied out at each floor level –

that is the wall line of one floor would project further out than the wall of the floor below it. In the medieval period these over-hangs could be quite wide, but the jetties became shallower by the end of the sixteenth century. The use of jetties was partly to improve the structural stability of the framing, partly to enable shorter posts to be used, and partly to increase the available floor space – although this seems to have been a fairly minor consideration. Eventually, jetties were also used partly for effect.

Timber-framing allowed for a great deal of ostentation, although the most elaborate framing developed in the late sixteenth century was mainly confined to the Midlands. By that time, Salisbury was stagnating and it has no buildings of that type. What it does have is a whole series of magnificently ornate wooden medieval roofs – over both timber-framed and stone buildings. Like much of medieval Salisbury, most of these are hidden from the general gaze because they are in private ownership.

24 A typical medieval timber-framed range on St John Street, probably dating to the fifteenth century. Two storeys, the first one jettied on plain bull-nosed jetty joists, its braced framing has typically large panels.

25 The Pheasant Inn, in Gore's Chequer on the corner of Salt Lane and Rolleston Street, is claimed to have been built in 1435 but was probably built later in that century. The gateway to the left leads through to the Shoemakers' Hall, built after 1638.

26 Over the Avon in the village of Harnham, the buildings were generally less expensively built – but none the less picturesque for that. The Rose and Crown Hotel has two separate buildings fronting the street. The far range is sixteenth century, but the one nearest the camera dates to the fourteenth century and has a crown-post roof. The buildings have clearly been restored and remodelled but much of the original work has survived.

27 Many of the old inn yards of Salisbury have gone, remodelled or built over. This fine staircase in the former yard of the Plume of Feathers off Queen Street is not quite what it seems. The lower part is Jacobean, the upper, curving part, early Georgian. It led to a gallery but the whole yard was radically rebuilt in the 1970s as part of a shopping centre.

Timber-framed buildings were not, originally, black and white; that is a Victorian misconception possibly based on the fact that the pitch and paint used to try and save the timbers of centuries-old buildings from rotting did result in this 'magpie' pattern. Incidentally, 'black-and-white' and 'half-timbered' are both terms that have no proper meaning when it comes to timber-framed buildings. Not a great deal is known about the external treatment of timber-framed buildings, but they were often gaudily painted in other parts of the country and Salisbury may have been even more colourful than it is now in centuries gone by.

Brick came early to Salisbury. In the 1540s it was being used for chimneys and for some decorative work in houses in the Close. Before 1610 a new brick wing had been added to the King's House in the Close prior to a visit by James I. A decade later, in the city, Cradock House, built on the site of a convent, was also largely built of brick. The bricks used in this period

28 The cheapest way to mask old-fashioned timber-framing was simply to render over the timbers. The two front gables of 91 Crane Street were built around the 1580s in front of even older buildings, and their rubble ground floor walls may be much older than the jettied timber-framed upper storeys. These were rewindowed and stuccoed at the beginning of the eighteenth century.

were typically dark red, hand-made, quite thin and, because they were fairly irregular, laid in thick mortar. By the latter part of the century the quality of brickwork had improved immensely, demonstrated by the Matron's College built just inside the Close's North Gate in 1682. From this period through to the nineteenth century, brick was the fashionable material to build in, unless you were wealthy enough to afford to encase your house in ashlar. The increasing use of brick coincided with the spread of neoclassical ideas that were gradually incorporated into the design of buildings. The busy multi-gabled buildings of the past gave way to symmetrical facades, sash windows and hidden roof lines; display and ostentation gave way to clarity of form and proportion.

The usual bricks in Salisbury's buildings are a lively red colour, but other hues were employed. In the later eighteenth century dark grey bricks were sometimes used for contrasting patterns or in the

29 One of the attractive features of Salisbury is its tile-hung buildings. This splendid example, in Swayne's Chequer on the corner of Pennyfarthing and Milford Streets, is essentially an early seventeenth-century timber-framed building jettied on each floor to each street. Until 1972 it had been covered with slate, but these were replaced by the more attractive tile.

30 Both slate and tile-hanging can be seen on the gables of these buildings in Oatmeal Row at the west end of the market place.

31 The tile-hanging tradition in Salisbury has never died out. In the nineteenth century, specially moulded tiles were produced just for this purpose, seen to good effect on this jettied timber-framed building by Ayleswade Bridge.

32 A more radical approach to updating timber-frames was to replace much of the panel infill with brick – or in this case, replace most of the areas between the main timbers with brick and stucco over. The recent stripping of the stucco from this house in Endless Street was obviously well intentioned but leaves a rather odd and not particularly pleasing impression. It simply was never meant to look like this.

blocking of 'blind' windows that kept the symmetry in façades where real glazed windows were not needed or did not fit with the internal arrangements. Such 'blind' windows, incidentally, were seldom the direct result of the window taxes.

For a short period from the end of the eighteenth century, another, and altogether less satisfactory, colour of brick was used. At this time London architects were using white bricks – though these were really a pale yellow. The fashion spread quickly, and by 1788 such bricks were being used in Salisbury's new Guild Hall. The fact that these 'whites' were seen to be more up to date than the local 'reds' can be seen in several houses whose back and side walls are of red brick, but whose facades are of 'white'. These yellow bricks can be used to effect in polychrome brickwork, contrasting with the reds or blues or greys, but when used in whole fronts they are rather dull and utilitarian, and do not age well.

33 Cradock House was built close to the site of a Franciscan convent established in 1230 and closed in 1538. The house, an early example of brick building in the city, is said to date from 1619 but it could well be earlier. The red bricks are small and hand-made, laid in a mainly English bond, with courses of bricks laid lengthways (stretchers) alternating with courses of bricks laid with their ends in the wall (headers).

34 By the end of the seventeenth century, brick construction and symmetry were the norm for any house of status. No. 49–51 High Street was for many years an inn and the brick front added in about the 1680s hid early work. The facade is a flattened 'E' shape, the bricks, now painted, decorated with ashlar.

After a brief vogue during the early nineteenth century for covering up brickwork with render lined to imitate stonework – stucco – brickwork re-emerged in the Victorian period. By this time the improvements in transport meant that it was possible to import bricks of widely different colours and textures from all over the country and gradually the local characteristics gave way to specialist mass-production. Another trend from the early nineteenth century was the painting of brickwork in pale or pastel hues – usually to the detriment of the building.

Closely allied to, and of greater antiquity than, the production of brick is the production of tile. Ceramic tiles were made in the early medieval period and long before then had probably covered some of the buildings of Sorviodunum. They were initially used as roof covering, especially after the use of thatch was banned by the city's authorities in the fifteenth century. Towards the end of the seventeenth century, many owners who could not afford to

35 By the time Vale House was built, on St Ann's Street, in 1784, the quality of brickwork had improved enormously and the symmetry of the age was simpler than it had been a century before. The brick bond is rather unusual, with a great deal of headers and few stretchers.

36 Not all of Salisbury's historic buildings are well cared for. This sorry specimen of late Georgian work on Exeter Street was formerly St Elizabeth's School, having been built as a rather fine family house. The wide windows on either side of the central bay have three portions – the central sashes flanked by much narrower ones. The technical term for this is 'tripartite' and it was a fashion that continued well into the nineteenth century.

37 In the south-east of England there was a development of tile-hanging that can deceive even the keenest eye. Mathematical tiles are actually tiles designed to look like bricks. This sixteenth-century timber-framed building, 30 Catherine Street, has slate-hanging on the side but mathematical tiles on the front – with an awkward junction at the corner. The building to the right is also faced with mathematical tiles, and is also timber-framed – but was probably built as late as the early nineteenth century.

rebuild their properties in the new-fangled brick rebuilt just their front walls. In Salisbury, and in the south-east of England in general, another method that protected the timber-framing and also gave the impression of being at least partly up to date was the use of tile-hanging. Battens were fixed to the frames and ordinary tiles hung from them. Usually these were laid square, but there are other examples of tiles laid in diagonals and later still especially shaped tiles were used as well. The uneven nature of the hand-made red tiles creates a rich, undulating and almost tactile surface and the tile-hung jettied timber-frames of Salisbury are amongst the most attractive buildings in the country – truly delightful. Later on, and adding yet more variety to the street scenes, slate-hanging enjoyed a degree of popularity.

Some of the brick fronts of Salisbury are not quite what they seem. When the overhanging upper floors of a building are faced with brick, there is obviously some cause for suspicion –

38 The doorway to Frowd's Almshouses, built in 1750 on Bedwin Street, was quite old fashioned for the date, with more than a hint of the English Baroque.

39 By the end of the eighteenth century 'white' (or yellow) bricks were in fashion – so mathematical tiles also became available to match. The front range of Windover House, on St. Ann's Street, was built by William Windover at the start of the seventeenth century. It was refaced in mathematical tiles about two centuries later and rewindowed.

40 Variations on tile and brick are terracotta or, as here, faience – a glazed tile popular in the late Victorian and Edwardian periods. This fine turn-of-the-century shop front is in green glazed tile and was added to a sixteenth-century timber-framed building in Fisherton Street.

41 The vogue for historic building styles has always been a feature of English architecture but was at no time stronger than in the nineteenth century. Salisbury's Odeon cinema has one of the finest interiors of any cinema anyway - as will be seen later. The pseudo-medieval front was added by local architect Frederick Bath in 1880.

or worry! Many buildings that appear to be of brick are, in fact, faced with a hybrid material – the so-called mathematical tile developed in the second half of the eighteenth century. This is, to all intents and purposes, a type of tile designed to look like a type of brick and often 'pointed' in the same manner after being nailed to the battens attached to the frames. The tiles were cleverly made and could replicate the various real brick bonds as well as the special high quality 'rubbed' bricks used over windows and doors. Mathematical tiles were made in a wide variety of colours, so in Salisbury there are both red and white examples. The purpose of this type of wall covering was simply to stay up with the latest architectural fashions without having to rebuild radically. Usually the brick tiles were fixed to timber-framed buildings, but there are rare examples, such as 47 Winchester Street, where a late seventeenth-century brick building has been recased in the tiles to appear more up to date,

41 The original fireplace is still in place in John Hall's hall, a fine specimen of medieval carving.

its windows and doors being altered at the same time. Apart from the fact that they are often used on jettied buildings, other clues to the use of mathematical tiles include slight slippages and uncertain junctions (or vertical planks) on corners – except those where the special corner tiles have been used.

One individual feature of Salisbury is the oriel window, seen in houses from the seventeenth century onwards but more typically used in the Georgian period. Usually at first, though sometimes at first and second, floor level, the wooden bays are canted and not the type of thing normally associated with the flat wall surfaces of brick Georgian buildings. They certainly add to the character of the city – and no doubt provide the houses' occupants with a good view both ways along the street.

The nineteenth century saw a gradual move away from the simplicity of neoclassical architecture to a rekindled interest in reviving the architectural styles of the past. This was seen more particularly in the Gothic Revival movement in ecclesiastic architecture and public buildings, but antique motifs were also used to decorate much humbler structures. This interest also led to a renewed interest in the real antique structures and in 1834 the great Gothic propagandist, A. W. N. Pugin, carried out one of the earliest sympathetic restorations of a medieval house – John Hall's, in New Canal. By the end of the century many frames, covered for centuries by plaster or tile-hanging, were restored and exposed to public gaze once again. The old had become not only acceptable, but desirable.

Sleepy Salisbury had experienced comparatively little growth in the nineteenth century and most of that was confined to the suburbs. There was thankfully little redevelopment in the centre of the medieval city, leaving its rich historic building stock comparatively intact. This, in turn, has helped the growth of Salisbury as a premier tourist attraction, and a general wish by locals and visitors alike to ensure that the city's ancient character is preserved.

Although the city has not had to suffer the often drastic redevelopments that have scarred too many historic towns and cities, there is no room for complacency. A few ugly modern buildings have been put up – such as the late 1960s buildings on Castle Street – and too many chequers are now little more than open car parks. One particularly inappropriate development has resulted in a large car park on the eastern

42 Cross Keys House, on the edge of the market place at the north-western corner of Cross Keys Chequer, was built in 1878 and was formerly the London & Liverpool Globe Insurance offices. The architect was H. Hall who is, not surprisingly, not very well known. The design certainly has a happy disregard for architectural history, but it certainly cannot be accused of lacking character.

43 The new shopping arcade behind the historic George Inn was built in the mid-1960s and is rather drab – however well intentioned and up-to-date its designers may have been for the time.

44 Modern architects can do it! This modern office block replaced derelict buildings on Milford Street. It is very long and low, but the facade is articulated by the boxy windows. Above all, thought has been given to the texture of the building – and why shouldn't a late twentieth century building be tile-hung?

edge of the city centre that has cut Culver Street in two and destroyed the adjacent chequer – a quite unnecessary erosion of an otherwise almost intact medieval street pattern. Another poor piece of planning has left one of the finest Georgian houses in the city, The Hall on New Street, isolated – a long, low and tedious multistorey car park begun in 1974 on one side and a modern office block on the other.

There has been a steady erosion of the smaller houses throughout the twentieth century, with all too many entries in the Royal Commission survey having the ominous phrase 'recently demolished'. In addition, Salisbury's buildings have suffered the usual problems of inappropriate shop fronts where former houses have been converted to commercial uses and, inevitably, the regretful loss of many multi-paned Georgian sashes and their replacement with characterless plate glass. In recent years things appear to be changing for the better. The new development behind the Town Mill – the Maltings – is, in parts, quite attractive and, given the problems facing public transport, the vast acreage of car park is obviously needed. Ultimately, it is up to the hard-working local pressure groups to continue to fight for their heritage, and to ensure that this remarkable city retains its position as one of the finest in Europe.

Castle and Defences

Both Old and New Salisbury were defended, though the defences of the new city were somewhat half-hearted. The Iron Age ditches around the hillfort were repaired on several occasions and then incorporated into the defences of the Norman castle shortly after the Conquest. In the middle of the enclosure King William ordered the construction of a huge earth mound, or 'motte', surrounded by a ditch, on top of which was the Great Tower, or keep. Other ditches from this motte running north and south divided the enclosure into two 'baileys'. Most of the original buildings and walls were built of timber, but the stone-built Great Tower and the East Gate may have been part of the first castle or built very soon afterwards. Certainly in the early twelfth century many other timber structures were were gradually replaced in stone in the time of Bishop Roger. This cleric, a friend and confidant of Henry I, controlled both cathedral and castle. At the time of his death in 1139 the north-eastern section of the new stone curtain wall on top of the prehistoric defences was unfinished – and never would be.

Bishop Roger may also have been responsible for the Courtyard House that can still be seen close by the Great Tower. It dates from the early twelfth century and consists of a great hall, great chamber, domestic buildings and the remains of a two-storey chapel block that once contained St Margaret's chapel on the ground floor, with St Nicholas's above. It was clearly a dwelling of some pretensions. By the end of the fourteenth century the castle had effectively been abandoned, and when John Leland visited it in Henry VIII's time he noted that 'ther

1 The Norman castle built within the ramparts of Old Sarum continued in use as an administrative centre and fortress for a century or so after the creation of the new city in the valley below, but was virtually derelict by the end of the fourteenth century. This is the base of its late eleventh-century Great Tower. The good quality ashlar of the sloping (or 'battered') plinth is original; the flint repair in the background is relatively modern and designed to show a little more of how the tower would have looked.

was a right fair and strong castelle within Old Saresbyri' but that only 'notable ruinus building of this castelle yet ther remayneth'.

Over the centuries since then the ruins were quarried further for building stone until it was taken into official care; it is now in the hands of English Heritage. All in all, there is not a great deal to see of the castle of Old Sarum, just a few low flint walls robbed of their ashlar facing – but it is one of the most atmospheric sites in the country. Over three hundred years ago, in 1668, Samuel Pepys reached the outskirts of Salisbury as night fell and wrote in his diary 'saw a great fortification . . . and to it and in it; and find it prodigious, so as to fright me to be in it all alone at that time of night, it being dark. I understand, since, it to be that, that is called Old Sarum.' Anyone visiting alone at night today would probably experience the same feelings of slight foreboding and solitude that Pepys felt – but in the daytime the views are splendid and the ghosts abed.

45 New Salisbury was allowed to have its own city defences, but little seems to have been done to build them. Odd portions of the earthen ram parts that were built survive in the grounds of the Council House in the north-eastern part of the city, probably retained simply as a garden feature for the house.

46 Despite only having earthern defences, the city did have masonry gates. This plaque, possibly dating to the 1630s, was re-erected in a wall in Castle Street in 1968. It was once part of the town's North, or Castle Street, Gate, taken down in 1788.

47 The boundary of the new Cathedral Close was originally marked by a water-filled ditch but in the early fourteenth century there was friction between the clergy and the townsfolk – a common occurrence at this time throughout England. Permission was given to demolish the old church at Old Sarum and use its stones to help in building a tall battlemented wall around the Close – much of which still survives. This portion is along Exeter Street, south of St Ann's Gate.

When the new city was laid out down below, there seems almost to have been a deliberate decision made not to hem it in with strong walls. The king had given permission for New Salisbury to be defended by adequate ditches in the royal charter of 1227. The city already had the natural defence of the Avon on the west and south sides, and all that was really needed were banks and ditches topped with palisades to the north and east. Little seems to have been done until the start of the fourteenth-century, and even then the work was not finished until well into the fifteenth century. Only two stone gateways were built, in Castle Street and Winchester Street. Leland noted that the city's ditch was 'thoroughly caste for the defence of the town but the waulle was never begun'. Within only a few years of the ditch and rampart being finished, the defences were allowed to fall into ruin, and most had been levelled by the early eighteenth century. Winchester Street Gate was

48 The North, or High Street, Gate to the Close still acts as a physical barrier between the city and the cathedral. This gate was built soon after the licence to fortify the Close was granted in 1327 and it is comparatively unaltered. The front, facing the High Street, was rebuilt a century or so later. At that time it was fitted with a portcullis, and although that is no longer there, its grooves can still be seen. The Royal Arms over the gateway were probably added to mark the Restoration of 1660.

3 St. Ann's Gate was probably begun in about 1327 but was extended shortly afterwards on at least two occasions and a chapel added above it. This room was later incorporated into Malmesbury House next door and traditionally is where Handel once played. The chapel windows are Victorian replacements, dated 1852.

demolished in 1771, followed ten years later by Castle Street Gate. All that is left of the defences today are sections of the rampart in the grounds of the Council House and a carved panel from the Castle Street Gate reset in a wall near where it stood.

From the very start of the city, the cathedral and its Close were totally separate from the secular world outside – no doubt a direct result of the conflicts at Old Sarum. At first the Close had no defences apart from water channels along its north and east sides. In the fourteenth century friction between church and people was quite common throughout England and led to the building of walls around many cathedral and monastic

complexes – both for defence and possibly to emphasize the power of the church. Those around the Close at Salisbury were begun after permission had been granted by the young Edward III in 1327, and a few years later the Dean and Chapter were allowed to demolish the remains of the old cathedral at Old Sarum and to reuse stones from it in the new wall. Several carved stones in the wall clearly came from the old site. Despite many changes and alterations, long stretches of the wall survive, complete, in parts with wall-walk and battlements. The main loss has been the west wall, which has virtually disappeared, and the north wall has been heavily rebuilt.

There were originally three gates through the Close wall, all finished by about 1350. The most important was that at the south end of the High Street, the main link between the city and its cathedral. The North Gate was probably started soon after permission had been given to build the Close wall. The internal arrangements are still identifiable, despite the alterations to the north side of the building in the fifteenth century when a new gateway was built, guarded by a portcullis. The decorated ashlared stonework provides a suitable terminus to the streetscape of timber-frames and brick.

To the east of the Close is St Ann's Gate, probably built at the same time as the North Gate. The construction breaks in the ashlared masonry show that it was altered several times in a short period. It possibly started off a simple postern gate through the wall, was then converted into a simple gatehouse, and, finally, extended westwards and given a large upper chamber initially used as a chapel dedicated to St Ann. It appears to have reached this stage by 1354. It later became part of a house and the chapel was sub-divided. The present west and east windows on the upper floor are of fourteenth-century style but of 1852 date.

Tucked away in the south-east corner of the Close is the South Gate, providing access to the Ayleswade Bridge and Harnham. This is a very simple structure, now minus its embattled parapet. Until fairly recently it was covered in picturesque ivy that was slowly clawing away at its ashlar and had to be removed.

In 1377 Bishop Erghum obtained permission from the king to 'crenelate' his palace to the south-east of the cathedral. This seems to have been the reason why an additional gateway was built in the east wall off Exeter Street. Unlike the other gates, it is built mainly of flint, a cheaper material than ashlar. It was also designed to be used as a reasonably high-status dwelling for one of the bishop's retainers, the tall gabled gateway section being flanked by lower wings on either side. It was the main entrance to the grounds of the Bishop's Palace, and is now used by the school.

Churches

New Salisbury was built to serve a new cathedral. Old Sarum had had a cathedral thrust upon it. Only the foundations of that cathedral within the hillfort remain, but even so these can tell a little of its architectural development. To get a better idea of the quality of the work a visit to the Salisbury museum in the Close to see the fragments of carved masonry on show is well worth while. Bishop Osmund, traditionally a nephew of King William and certainly his Chancellor and Keeper of the Great Seal, took office in 1078. He was responsible for the first church, started shortly afterwards. Consecrated in April 1092 it was struck by lighting five days later and badly damaged. It had quite an odd ground plan, with a fairly standard aisled nave but a chancel with exceedingly narrow aisles and short, stubby transepts; it was also very small for a cathedral.

Osmund died in 1099 and after a period when there was no bishop Bishop Roger took over, radically enlarged the church and finished the claustral buildings attached to it. His masterplan was halted when he became embroiled in the civil war between Stephen and Matilda, and his vast lands were confiscated in the 1130s. The removal of the bishop's 'cathedra', or chair, to the new church in the valley less than a century later inevitably led to the gradual decline of the old cathedral, although a chapel within it was still being used well into the thirteenth century. Masonry from the church buildings and canons' houses was used in the repairs of the castle, but only in 1331 was the great church demolished completely to provide masonry for the new wall around the Close of its successor. There were several other churches and chapels in Old Sarum, but no traces of them survive.

Mass was first said in the tiny wooden chapel down in the river meadows in 1219 and work began on the new church of

2 The clarity of architectural purpose in the magnificent Early English interior of Salisbury owes, in some ways, as much to James Wyatt as it does to the medieval architectural genius who designed it. Wyatt's ruthless 'architectural cleansing' swept all before it as he reinterpreted the medieval past. Quite what Elias de Dereham or Nicholas of Ely would have thought is another matter.

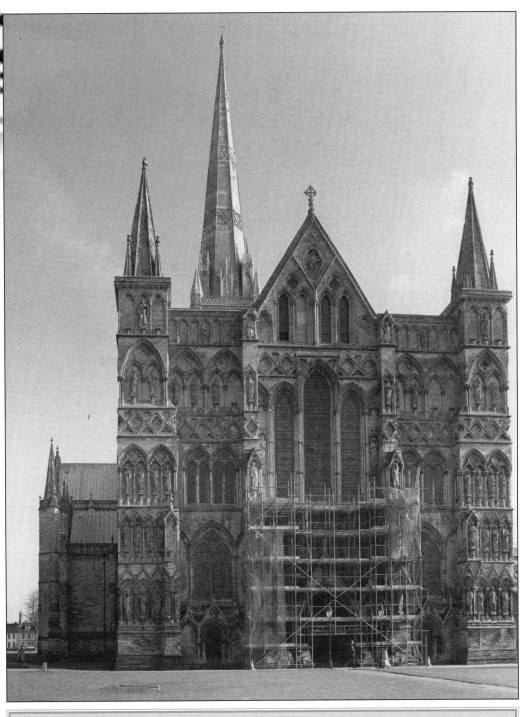

2 The great medieval cathedrals often took centuries to complete and for most of the time were also being remodelled. A cathedral today without scaffolding and ongoing appeals for repair funds is very much a rarity – and so little has changed. The is the west end of the cathedral in 1994.

Our Lady the Blessed Virgin Mary in the following year. In overall charge was Elias de Dereham, who was also involved in the building of Winchester Castle and a new chapel at Clarendon Palace. His house, Leadenhall, on the west side of the Close was the first to be built and acted as a model for the other canonical houses; sadly its last remains were destroyed in 1915. The master mason was Nicholas of Ely, and he was probably responsible for the design. Elias appears to have been the equivalent of a project officer or clerk of works, and Nicholas the architect. In 1225 the Trinity Chapel could be consecrated and the following year the bodies of three former bishops, including St Osmund, were transferred from the old church to the new. By 1237 the entire east end was finished. In 1246 Nicholas and Elias both died, but within twenty years the great church was finished. To build a cathedral of this size in less than fifty years was a remarkable achievement, and it is the

2 The stalls of the cathedral are splendid examples of craftsmanship in wood. Although they look Victorian, much of the thirteenth-century carpentry survives, along with many original misericords. The organ case is by George Street and the canopies, designed by Sir Arthur Blomfield, were in place by 1925.

very fact that it was built in such a short time that gives to Salisbury its unique feeling of architectural purity and oneness. Some have nothing but admiration for its completeness; others are chilled by its almost mechanical perfection. The top of the tower and the spire, it is true, are later additions, but ones that are in happy accord with the rest.

Set splendidly in the crisply-cropped greensward of its huge Close, Salisbury is the definitive masterpiece of that first truly native form of the Gothic style – the aptly named Early English. It is a style characterized by height and narrowness, by soaring interiors lined by slender columns and lit by tall lancet windows. Built mostly of good quality limestone brought from Chilmark, its plan is very simple and has not been altered to any great extent by later changes. It consists of nave, crossing, transepts and an east end almost as long as the west with its own shorter choir transepts. To the south are the

2 The cloister is the earliest, and largest, of any English cathedral. The slender arcading has had to be restored many times and as early as the seventeenth century Wren had to improve the buttresses. This is is east walk, above which is the library, begun in the 1440s. It once covered the whole walk, but the southern half was taken down in the Georgian period.

cloisters and the chapter house – and being a secular cathedral there were no monastic buildings.

Externally, only the west end, the great show front of the church, can occasionally feel dislocated from the overall design. It is, perhaps, a bit too pompous and a little too rich with statuary, and also has something of the stage set about it, being wider than the church behind it. This apparent need to embellish the west fronts of cathedrals can sometimes detract from our modern appreciation of their aesthetic qualities but has to be accepted as part and parcel of their medieval architecture. The rest is as perfect a specimen of the Gothic style as England can provide and it is difficult to quibble with Sir Christopher Wren's opinion that it 'may be justly accounted one of the best patterns of architecture in that age wherein it was built'.

It is unclear whether or not the original design of the

2 An internal view of the east walk of the Cloister, showing how the elegant simplicity of the arcading is reflected in the answering blank arcade of the opposite wall and in the vaulting. Midway along on the right is the entrance to the Chapter House.

2 The religious and official life of the cathedral was mainly carried out in the octagonal Chapter House, built in the 1280s and influenced by the one recently finished at Westminster. Light and airy, it has a central column to help support the vaulting inside. Around the inside is a stone bench and a blind arcade, above which are a series of stone-carved Bible stories.

cathedral included a taller tower, or a spire. The structural evidence certainly suggests that nothing as ambitious as the existing tower and the spire was first planned, and that it would have had a lantern topped by a light low spire made of wood. When the decision was made to raise the tower and add the stone spire, considerable alterations had to be made to the top of the existing tower to take the weight of the additional masonry – estimated to be as much as 6,500 tons. These were not entirely successful, as the straining arches added over the years to all the transepts and the obvious settlement of piers around the crossing clearly show. The spire itself is octagonal, and the junction between it and the tower is handled with architectural dexterity and skill. Towards the top of the spire the stone work is only inches thick. Inside is the original wooden scaffolding, deliberately left to brace the structure. A windlass to carry up the stones is also still in place. The top of the spire is 180 ft above the top of the tower, and 404 ft above ground level – making it, now, the tallest in Britain. The odd thing is that no one really knows when this well-known and much-loved engineering masterpiece was built. The style is different to that of the rest of the church, in the developed form of English Gothic known as Decorated. This came in towards the end of the thirteenth century and the date usually given for the start of the spire is 1334. The ball-flower encrusted tower is very similar to towers built during the first half of the fourteenth century at Pershore and Hereford. However, recent research seems to indicate that the work is a little earlier, and that it was finished by 1300. Since then it has dominated the surrounding countryside and in 1668 the diarist Pepys was not the first, nor the last, to be guided 'all over the plain by the sight of the steeple'. It is one of the crowning glories of English architecture.

Inside the cathedral the first impression is that the unity evident outside is continued within; it is the finest Early English interior in the world. Some may quibble with the repetitiveness of the design and others lament the lack of surprise in that repetitiveness. More seriously, perhaps, is the often-voiced complaint that the triforium arches are too squat for the height of the walls, and that the continuous string course below interrupts the verticality of the design.

2 A detail of the painted vaulting above the choir. The original paintings were limewashed at the Reformation and these rather indifferent copies are by the firm of Clayton & Bell. They date to the time of Gilbert Scott's restoration.

50 The small parish church of Harnham, dedicated to St George, was probably a century or so old by the time the new cathedral was started on the other side of the Avon. It was a simple church with a nave and small chancel, both of which survive relatively intact. The major additions have been a fourteenth-century south chapel and the tower-porch on the north side, rebuilt in the 1830s in a chequer pattern of flint and brick.

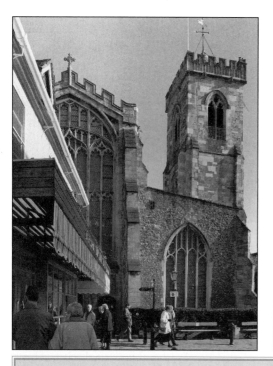

51 When New Salisbury was first laid out, a church was built at the west ern end of the huge market place to cater for the spiritual needs of those in the city centre. St Thomas's has since been hemmed in by later building, and now stands in its own intimate square. Only fragments of the first church survive and the rest is mainly of later fifteenth century date – and a fine example of a Perpendicular Gothic 'Wool' church. This rebuilding was not just an act of pious renewal by its wealthy parishioners; the old chancel had fallen down in 1448! The interior of St Thomas's is particularly fine, with superb late fifteenth century roofs. This is the west end of the north aisle.

Nevertheless, Salisbury exudes a feeling of light and delicacy throughout its entire 473ft length, helped by the contrast between the light Chilmark stone and the burnished Purbeck marble.

To the south of the church are the cloisters, the largest and earliest of any cathedral in Britain, begun in the 1260s in a very early version of the Decorated style, the Geometric. To allow light to reach the south windows of the nave, a gap was left between the north walk of the cloisters and the church, a gap now occupied by the cathedral's tea rooms and shop. In the design, everything is uniform again, the slender shafts of the claustral arcades are quite splendid. There are still signs of the glazing grooves in the surrounds. The fine Chapter House, with its central clustered column, was built around 1280 and copied from the one at Westminster Abbey.

The cathedral we see today is more like it was in the fourteenth century than it had become by the eighteenth. By then, two chantry chapels had been added to either side of the Trinity Chapel, and a variety of tombs and altars were scattered about the interior. Outside, the Close was partly taken up by the headstones of the graveyard. The cathedral had suffered during the upheaval of the Reformation, and again during the Commonwealth, when bishops were abolished and it became just another parish church. All in all it was not in a particularly good condition. Sir Christopher Wren had been called in by Bishop Seth Ward in the late seventeenth-century to advise on repair work and, a century later, James Wyatt, one of the most famous architects of his day, restored the cathedral. Reviled as 'the Destroyer' by later historians, Wyatt demolished the chantry chapels (although that was not his decision), and tidied up the tombs of the interior, as well as levelling the Close and demolishing the battered remains

52 By the time it was decided that a third parish church was needed for the thriving new city, in 1269, the only land available was on the north-eastern fringe of the main part of it. St Edmund's was a huge church, and was collegiate – supporting a team of priests that lived in the adjacent college. The present building is essentially just the chancel of the original church; the crossing tower fell in 1653 and the nave was demolished soon afterwards when a replacement tower was built.

of the detached thirteenth-century bell tower to the north. He was certainly quite ruthless, but also had a set idea of how the medieval cathedral should look – and it is his vision, by and large, that we see today, despite later work by Sir George Gilbert Scott between 1860 and 1875. At this time one complaint about the cathedral was that it was so cold, a fact that the installation of the patent 'Gurney' stoves in the last century failed to remedy properly. John Ruskin, the great Victorian art critic, blamed any imperfections of his famous book *The Severn Lamps of Architecture* on catching a chill in Salisbury cathedral! A new and better heating system has been one of the benefits of the major restoration work that has taken place throughout much of

54 St Martin's served a small village clustered around it and, probably, Milford, a settlement further west. Whilst it was founded long before New Salisbury, the oldest part of the present building – the chancel – was probably started at the same time as the cathedral. The huge aisled nave was built in the fifteenth century in the Perpendicular style then fashionable – a typical remodelling paid for by the wool trade.

the twentieth century – and which is still continuing. Only through such constant maintenance can this superb cathedral be preserved for future generations.

For a prosperous medieval city Salisbury had surprisingly few medieval churches. Nearby Winchester, in comparison, had nearly sixty churches when Salisbury was being laid out. By the thirteenth century more attention was being given by the authorities to canon law, reducing the proliferation of tiny parishes. Also, because it was a planned city, the spiritual needs of its inhabitants could be carefully calculated. In other towns of similar status growth was often haphazard and organic, and many separate parishes, often quite small, developed. Salisbury, in the medieval period, had just three fairly populous parishes, all capable of building fine churches – and all three were radically rebuilt at a time when Salisbury was at the height of its fortunes, in the fifteenth century. This

55 The medieval parish church of Fisherton Anger was St Clement's, sited not far from the River Nadder. The arrival of the railways in the mid nineteenth century led to a rapid growth of a new suburb slightly further north and west, and in 1852 a new church was opened to serve it and St Clement's was pulled down. St Paul's was designed by Thomas Henry Wyatt, but the new roundabout does little for it.

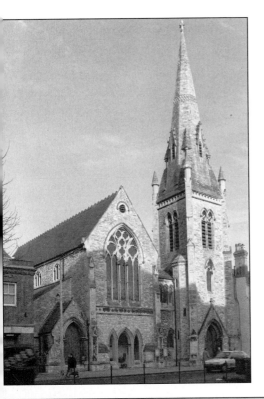

56 Looking for all the world like a typical neo-Gothic Victorian suburban parish church, this is the former Congregationalist church on Fisherton Street, begun in 1878 to the designs of Tarring and Wilkinson.

57 The great John Wesley himself offered advice on the first Methodist chapel in St Edmund's Church Street, but that 1759 building was rebuilt in 1811. It was extended towards the street in 1835 and this elevation was later rendered. Inside the galleries are supported on wooden columns, and altogether the chapel could hold 800 people.

meant they were also all rebuilt or remodelled in the last true native phase of English Gothic – the so-called Perpendicular, with its large wide windows and tall interiors.

At least two of the existing settlements on the edges of the new city already had churches before the bare-footed Bishop Poore laid the first foundation stone of the new cathedral in 1220. The oldest and most complete is the small church of St George's, just over the Avon in Harnham. The church, mainly constructed of flint, had a fairly plain nave and chancel by the twelfth century, was remodelled in succeeding centuries and restored in the mid-nineteenth century. The tower porch on the north side probably has fourteenth-century origins but was largely rebuilt in the early nineteenth century in an attractive brick-and-flint chequered pattern.

The village to the east of the new city, St Martin's, probably had a church by the mid-eleventh century which also served nearby Milford. The oddly aligned masonry low down in the west end of the nave may belong to that early foundation. The style of the chancel is a much humbler version of the Early English used for the cathedral, and it was probably built at about the same time as the new cathedral was begun. Built mainly in flint, it has typically tall lancet windows. The rest of the church was largely rebuilt in the fourteenth and fifteenth centuries, the offset tower and spire predating the spacious nave and aisles. The church was restored in 1849, when the present east windows were added, and again, at a cost of over £3,000, in 1886.

To serve the spiritual needs of the first citizens of New Salisbury, a chapel of ease was built at the west end of the huge market place. The church of St Thomas of Canterbury was certainly in existence by the 1230s, but only tiny fragments of this first building survive, in the east wall. Most of the present church dates from the second half of the fifteenth century, after the collapse of the old chancel in 1448. The unusually positioned south tower is slightly earlier, built in about 1400 and originally separate from the rest of the church. By this time the churchyard had been largely built over and the once spacious site in the market place was now a rather crowded square.

Apart from the fine low-pitched timber roofs, the most notable feature of the church is the magnificent 'Doom' painted over the chancel arch in around 1500. Wall-paintings often covered most of the interiors of churches; they were the

God...now commandeth all men everywhere to repent

58 The former Methodist chapel in the Wilton Road, with its rather sweet curved portico, opened in 1880. It is now an Emmanuel church.

way of getting the Word across to the vast majority of their congregations who couldn't read. The 'Dooms' reinforced the church's teaching or threat of hell and damnation to those who failed to toe the line, and were deliberately placed for the maximum effect. In the Reformation, wall-paintings were considered to be papist and superstitious, and were defaced and whitewashed over. Such was the fate of the paintings of St Thomas's, but they were exposed briefly at the start of the nineteenth century and restored during the renovation work of 1881. The church is again undergoing expensive repairs in the 1990s.

The rapid growth of New Salisbury led to the need for a new parish church, and St Edmund's was founded to the north-east of the centre in 1269. It was a collegiate church, that is, it supported a team of priests headed by a provost. The college itself, where the priests were housed, was on the site now occupied by the Council House. Nothing obvious remains of the original church, and only the broad nave and its aisles are medieval. These were built at the very start of the fifteenth century and were originally at the east end of what must have been a very large church. The present nave was once the chancel and the aisles on either side of it were the St John and Lady chapels. That church had a central tower over the crossing, transepts and a nave to the west. In June 1653 the churchwarden's accounts describe how during one Sunday service 'the walles of the Tower thereof were becoming ruinous ... [and] ... Broken ... the main pillars did bulge out, and sensibly shake: the cleftes in the walles were seen to open and shutt with ringing of the Sermon Bell ...'. On the following day the tower of the then empty church collapsed, although no one was hurt. The nave was also in a bad state of repair and it was decided to demolish it. The tower was rebuilt in a medieval style and became the west tower of a much truncated church. In the mid-eighteenth century a new chancel was built to the east, but this was replaced by the present chancel in 1865 – built by Sir George Gilbert Scott, who also lengthened the aisles. The tower was restored in 1889. The church became ecclesiastically redundant in 1973 and now houses an arts centre.

One other medieval chapel should be mentioned, for it is a rare survival. It is also very difficult to appreciate exactly what it is. Medieval bridges were often maintained by both tolls and by the rents of lands endowed to small chapels built on the bridges to cater for the needs of wayfarers. Ayleswade Bridge (or Harnham Bridge) was built in the 1240s. It is made up of two sections, and on the island in the middle Bishop Bingham built the bridge chapel of St John's. Astonishingly, it has survived almost intact, despite being converted to secular uses centuries ago. It has been a house since at least the eighteenth century, and its rendered walls hide most of its architectural secrets.

After the end of the medieval period, Salisbury experienced

59 The Baptists were active in Salisbury in the late seventeenth century and established a chapel on Brown Street in 1719. The present building was put up in 1860, faced with a rather harsh red brick.

little or no growth in population and needed little or no expansion in its church provision. However, in the nineteenth century the city began to expand. The growth of Fisherton after the arrival of the railways led to a need for a new church in that area. There was an old village church, St Clement's, a little to the south of the station but it was considered too small and too decrepit. It was decided to build a new one further north, and the dedication was changed to St Paul. Designed by Thomas Henry Wyatt, an Irish first cousin of the more famous architect James Wyatt, it is in the Early English style and was opened in 1852. Old St Clement's was then pulled down. The north aisle was added in 1876. It is a rather pleasing church but its setting

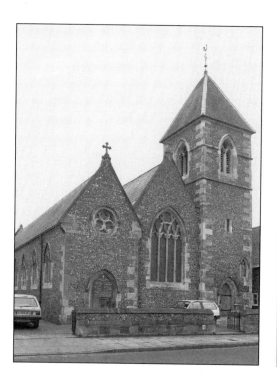

60 A guide book published soon after St Osmund's was built referred to it as the 'handsome Catholic church on Exeter Street'. It is, though, a rather plain church and notable only as being one of the last works of Augustus Welby Northmore Pugin, finished in 1848 shortly before his final lapse into insanity and his all too early death in 1852. The addition of the over-long north aisle in 1894 ruined Pugin's composition.

has been destroyed by the construction of a busy roundabout right next to it.

At the opposite side of the city is another Victorian suburban church suffering badly from the same 'roundabout blight' – St Mark's, on the London Road. The architect was J. A. Reeve and the church opened in 1892. The type of Gothic Revival used in this design is, very unusually, Perpendicular. The church is surprisingly long, faced with rock-cut stone and dominated by a somewhat low and brooding crossing tower. It looks as if this tower was designed to be higher but was never finished. Nevertheless, overall the design is very effective but its true qualities are ruined by the blighted setting.

There have been nonconformist places of worship in the city since the seventeenth century, but few of their chapels possess much of architectural worth. The two principal exceptions

were opened within a year of each other to very different designs. In 1878 work began on a new Congregationalist church in Fisherton Street designed by the little-known partnership of Tarring and Wilkinson. Opened in the following year, it cost £7,000. It is a bold, but strange, version of the neo-Gothic being used in orthodox Church of England suburban churches in the Victorian period. In this particular case the style is vaguely Early Decorated (typical of the later thirteenth and early fourteenth centuries), and the church has nave, aisles and an apse. The spire is 132 ft high.

More in keeping with the neoclassical tradition of nonconformity is the Italianate former Methodist chapel on the Wilton Road, now used as an Emmanuel church. Architecturally inaccurate it may be, but it has not a little charm – especially in its curving portico. Opened in 1880 it could hold 400 people; the architect seems to be unknown.

61 The disused Methodist chapel in Milford Street was started in 1896 and is no architectural triumph. The debased Italianate style is a triumph of money over taste. Is it worth saving?

The great cathedral of Salisbury was, of course, built as a Roman Catholic place of worship and remained so until the great upheavals of Henry VIII's reign. Catholics were not allowed real freedom of worship until the Catholic Emancipation Act and it was some time after that that the present Roman Catholic church of St Osmund's was built facing the Close wall in Exeter Street. It was dedicated to the builder of the first cathedral on Old Sarum. One of the principal benefactors was John Lambert, who asked his friend Augustus Welby Pugin, the most famous proponent of the Gothic Revival and a one-time resident of Salisbury, to design it. It has to be said that the church, begun in 1847 and one of Pugin's last works, is something of a disappointment. It was enlarged in 1894.

As well as the College of St Edmund's and the Bridge Chapel of St John's, the city also had other religious foundations in the medieval period. Both the Greyfriars (Franciscans) and the Blackfriars (Dominicans) had houses in Salisbury in the thirteenth century. The Franciscans occupied a site off St Ann's Street in 1228, and the Dominicans moved to Salisbury from Wilton in 1281. Both were closed at the Dissolution and nothing survives of either.

Public Buildings

New Salisbury has always been an important regional centre and effectively wrested control of the county from Wilton soon after it was founded. Until the early seventeenth century the city was still controlled by the bishop, whose guild hall was built in the market place as a continual reminder of the fact. Despite this, in the late sixteenth century the city's council had built their own council house nearby. In 1780 it was badly damaged by fire and plans were started to replace it with a new one. Renamed the Guild Hall, the new structure was built on the site of the medieval bishops' guild hall, which was pulled down to make room for it; the last vestige of the bishop's former power was removed in the process.

The original design of the Guild Hall was by Sir Robert Taylor, who died in the year that work started – 1788. The actual construction was therefore entrusted to one of his pupils, William Pilkington, who altered some aspects of the design – notably the main windows. In 1829 it was altered and extended by Thomas Hopper and was described shortly afterwards as 'a substantial and handsome building of white brick, ornamented with rustic quoins and cornices of stone'. That view may seem odd today. The yellowing 'white bricks' seem far too cheap a material for such a prestigious building, and warm red bricks would have been far better if stone was considered too expensive. There is a lack of cohesion in the design and a certain heavy-handedness of detail that detracts from any inherent qualities the design may have had. Salisbury's market place deserved better.

Confusingly, there is also now a Council House in Salisbury again, this time away from the centre of the town. Although the building dates back to the sixteenth century, it has only been the Council House since 1927. After the College of St Edmund's next to the church was closed by order of Henry VIII in 1546 the buildings and land eventually came into the hands of Giles Estcourt. He seems to have built a new house on the site of the demolished medieval buildings. At the Restoration in 1660 'The College' was bought by the Wyndham family who had the symmetrical south front refaced in brick in the mid eighteenth century, and in 1790 Samuel Pepys Cockerell designed a north wing. In the late nineteenth century it passed out of the Wyndham family and in 1873 became a school. Then, in 1927, the council bought the property to mark the 700th anniversary of the city's first charter and it is now used as council offices. In the grounds,

62 The foundation stone for Sir Robert Taylor's Guild Hall was laid on 14 October 1788. Taylor's design was altered during construction, and then again in 1829 when the formerly recessed entrance portico in the main elevation was replaced by the present unsatisfactory arrangement with its projecting portico and ugly first floor windows. The Guild Hall was built on the site of the fourteenth-century bishop's guildhall, the last reminder of the former power of the prelate over the city.

now a public park, is a fifteenth-century porch that once protected the north door of the cathedral's north transept. This Perpendicular Gothic addition was considered by James Wyatt to be out of character with the rest of the cathedral when he was restoring it in the 1790s, but it was rescued by the Wyndhams. They had it carefully dismantled and rebuilt in their garden as a folly in 1791, embellishing it with an unconvincing spire.

From the very beginning of the new city its market was of crucial importance. The market place was then larger and different commodities were sold in different parts of it. Often these individual trading areas had their own market crosses – possibly quite simple structures at first, they developed into quite elaborate and expensive ones. Salisbury is fortunate to have its Poultry Cross still standing. The first cross would have been at the south-western corner of the original market place.

63 The prosaically named Council House was bought by the city in 1927 and converted to office use – hence its name. The present building began as a large house built soon after the ancient College of St Edmund's was dissolved in the mid sixteenth century. That house was given its present symmetric south front in the mid eighteenth century and a north wing was added in 1790. By that time it was the finest and largest house outside the Close.

5 The fifteenth-century Poultry Cross at the corner of Butcher Row and Minster Street was one of at least four market crosses that once stood in the city. Most of the upper portions were designed by the Winchester ar chitect Owen Browne Carter and built in 1852–4.

The present cross was probably built of Chilmark ashlar some time in the fifteenth century, but its present appearance owes much to a restoration in the mid-nineteenth century. Before that time the cross had lost its upper portion, and all of the present work above the balustrade was added during 1852–4.

In an attempt to revitalize the market after the arrival of the railways, a new market house (soon to be called the Corn Exchange) was built at the west side of the market place and officially opened on 24 May 1859. Although described at the time as 'in form an ancient Roman basilica', it was a very plain and utilitarian building, the walls built of brick and the inside of cast-iron and glass. Only the ashlar-faced facade to the market place aspired to grandeur – designed by the chief engineer of the London & South Western Railway, John Strapp. The railway connection was also a physical one – a small branch line linked the Corn Exchange to the sidings near the station. The front

64 The ashlar-faced former Corn Exchange of 1859 now fronts the city's library, and has done since 1975. Most of the interior of the original building has been swept away. Designed by John Strapp, the exchange was linked by its own railway line to the main line at Fisherton. For many years after the Second World War it seemed doomed to demolition, but at least part has been saved and it serves its new function well.

65 Most of the craft guilds had their own halls in which to meet and entertain. The Joiners' Hall on St Ann's Street was built after 1617 when several smaller guilds combined. Later converted into a pair of houses it was restored by the National Trust after they acquired it at the end of the last century.

survives as the main entrance to the new library built in the mid 1970s. Most of the rest of the building was pulled down in 1974 as part of the project. Usually this 'facadism' is to be regretted – it is not honest architecture. However, there are always exceptions to any rule and in this case the right decision was taken to retain a little piece of Salisbury's nineteenth-century past and give it a twentieth-century purpose.

Individual craft guilds had their own guild halls scattered around the city. Until 1971 three of these still stood, but in that year the sadly neglected Tailors' Hall off Pennyfarthing Street was demolished; it had been built in the early sixteenth century. The other two halls are less ancient. Several trade guilds combined in 1617 to form the Joiners' Guild, and they built their new guild hall at the east end of St Ann's Street. Its finest features are the tall oriel windows lighting the original first floor hall. By the nineteenth century it had been converted

into two houses and was falling into disrepair. In 1898 it was saved by the fledgeling National Trust who have looked after it since. It is, however, not open to the public but rented out.

In 1638 Philip Crewe, a schoolmaster, left his fifteenth-century house on Salt Lane to the Shoemaker's Company with the wish that they would 'inlarge and make my said dwelling house or some pte thereof' into their guild hall and name it after him. Crewe's Hall still stands though it is known as the Shoemaker's Guild-hall. The guild built a new timber-framed extension to the house, with a hall on the first floor above a kitchen. The schoolmaster's house later became the Crispin Inn, named after the patron saint of shoemakers, but it is now called the Pheasant.

Part of the role of the medieval church was to look after the poor and the sick. One quite remarkable survival of such medieval welfare stands just north of Ayleswade Bridge. St Nicholas's Hospital was founded, or possibly refounded, by

66 The walk down to Ayleswade Bridge is worth taking if only to see the remarkable remains of St Nicholas's Hospital, one of the few thirteenth-century hospitals still surviving. Its original role of caring for the sick and the poor evolved into that of almshouses – and it is still in use as such. It is also said to have been the inspiration for Hiram's hospital in Trollope's first Barsetshire Chronicle – *The Warden*.

67 The Infirmary on Fisherton Street has only just closed after more than two centuries of service to the city. Its only architectural claim to fame is in being probably the worst building designed by an otherwise fine architect – John Wood the younger of Bath. However, it is sad to see it closed and derelict – and surely there must be a use for it.

Bishop Bingham in about 1231 when the oldest portion of the complex was begun. The design is interesting. The main range, built of flint with stone decoration, was originally a wide single-storey structure with a central arcade dividing it into two halves. At the east end, each half had its own chapel, and at the west, its own porch. It has been suggested that one half was for men and the other for women – though privacy would have been rather lacking. Later, most of the northern half was demolished, leaving the arcade exposed in the rebuilt portion. To the north is another, smaller building, running parallel to the main block. This may have been part of the original hospital but its function is unknown. It may have been the home of those tending the sick. The hospital was restored by William Butterfield in the mid nineteenth century.

Like most medieval cities, Salisbury suffered from sporadic outbreaks of plague, smallpox and cholera. After the Reformation, most charities were secular in nature and often of small scale and with few resources. Concerns with the nation's health in the eighteenth century led to the establishing of new hospitals in larger towns, and in the 1760s proposals were put forward for one in Salisbury. In 1767 John Wood the Younger, of Bath, provided designs for a general infirmary on Fisherton Street. This was the John Wood responsible for the famous Royal Crescent in his home town, but the Salisbury Infirmary was a much plainer affair – in fact, it borders on the downright dull. The foundation stone was laid in the September of 1767 and it was officially opened on 17 August 1771. Described once as 'that great, comely building of warm red brick', it now seems forbidding and austere. Stripped of ornament, any classical proportions were ruined by its height and the evident need to have taller windows on the upper floor than on the one below it. The rear and side walls are still topped by rather silly brick battlements. Much extended over the years, the Infirmary continued to fulfil the purposes for which it was designed until 1993. Now the buildings are empty and awaiting new uses.

Long before the creation of the welfare state the poor as well as the sick often suffered appalling hardships. Private charities helped as much as they could but Salisbury early on tried to help – albeit in the less-than-liberal ways of the seventeenth century. Church House on Crane Street became a workhouse in 1634 and remained so for nearly two hundred and fifty years. Originally the inmates were housed in the medieval building, but in 1728 a new block was built along the south side of the courtyard in brick and with typical early Georgian detailing. On the ground floor was a huge open workshop, and the inmates presumably lived on the upper floors.

The only grimmer places than the workhouse were the prisons. The county gaol remained in the castle at Old Sarum for many years after the cathedral had closed and must have been a grim place indeed. The new city gaol, from the sixteenth century onwards, stood close by the Fisherton

68 Tucked away in the courtyard behind Church House on Crane Street is the tall brick former workhouse built in 1728, a building that no doubt struck terror into the hearts of the unemployed and the needy. Church House itself had become the city's workhouse as early as 1638. The complex is now owned by the Church – hence the name.

69 High Victorian Gothic at its most garish, the Literary and Scientific Institution on New Street certainly cannot be accused of being bland. Dated 1871 it is the work of A. Bothams.

70 The grim city gaol by Fisherton Bridge was built in the sixteenth century but was rebuilt in the Georgian period. Demolished in the early nineteenth century, fragments of walling survive under Dr Roberts's clock tower, a memorial to his wife, Arabella, unveiled in 1893.

71 The foundation stone of the former library on Chipper Lane was laid in November 1904, and the building was partly paid for by a grant by the philanthropist Andrew Carnegie. Since 1975 the library has been housed in the former Corn Exchange and the old building, restored in 1989, has found new uses. The Young Gallery to the left was added in 1913 to house the art collection of Edwin Young.

Bridge. It was extended in 1783 but closed in 1822 when a new county gaol (long since demolished) was opened. Briefly used as part of the adjacent Infirmary, the buildings were all but demolished by the mid nineteenth century. Part of the ashlared wall of the 1783 block survives still, and on it in 1892 a Dr Roberts paid for the construction of the vaguely Gothic clock tower as a memorial for his wife, Arabella. It is a little 'Big Ben' built on the cheap.

Education, albeit to a favoured few usually destined for the clergy, was also a responsibility of the church and the Cathedral School of St Mary the Virgin is possibly older than the city itself, traditionally founded alongside the first cathedral at Old Sarum. Since 1947, part of its accommodation is, suitably, in the medieval former Bishop's Palace in the Close. After the Reformation, education passed mainly into secular hands and enjoyed a great revival in the nineteenth

72 Appropriately enough, Salisbury has a theological college, on the north side of the Close. The main portion is a typically symmetrical late seventeenth-century house with projecting wings built in the late 1670s. In 1860 it became a theological college and new buildings were added to the rear. These were by William Butterfield, who also designed the chapel to the right, opened in 1881.

73 In the eighteenth century, with the improvements in the road system, Salisbury became an important staging centre and had several well-known inns. The White Hart Hotel gives its name to the chequer but its 1820s block faces St John's Street. The bold Ionic portico, topped by a statue of a hart, gives this nine-bay facade the look of a minor country house.

74 Above this shop at the corner of New Canal and High Street, the large arched windows once lit the Assembly Rooms, built in 1802. Briefly a fashionable rendezvous for Salisbury society, they are now used for storage.

century. None of Salisbury's later schools are of particular architectural worth – but the size of some of the surviving national schools attached to churches was surprisingly large. For example, St Edmund's National School could hold 500 pupils when it was built in 1860.

Allied with the education of children was education in general, particularly promoted at the turn of the twentieth century in the provision of libraries. The Scottish-born multi-millionaire Andrew Carnegie was an advocate of library provision and gave out grants to help build them. One of those to benefit from his charity was the library in Salisbury,

75 The front of the Red Lion Hotel in Milford Street was built at about the same time as the White Hart but clearly visible through the driveway is evidence of much earlier construction. Some buildings around its courtyard date back to the fourteenth century.

76 In the nineteenth century banks became an increasingly important part of everyday life, and their architecture began to reflect their status in the world. Lloyds Bank on Blue Boar Row is typical. The original five bay section, of 1869, is to the left, with a segmental pediment under the sculpture. The wider five bays to the right were added in the same Venetian Gothic palace style in 1901.

originally opened in 1890. In 1904 a grant by Carnegie and money raised by public subscription paid for a purpose-built library on Chipper Lane. It was designed in a vaguely neo-Tudor style by A. C. Bothams. Next door to it, in 1913, Edwin Young paid for a new gallery, designed by a Mr Blount, to hold his art collection. Neither buildings are architectural masterpieces, and both have found new uses after being restored in 1989. Nevertheless, both provided an important service to the city for many years. An equally undignified piece of educational architecture, also by A. Bothams, is the over-elaborate polychromatic-brick High Victorian Gothic Literary & Scientific Institute opened on New Street in 1871.

Houses

The ruins of the oldest, and in its time no doubt one of the finest, houses in Salisbury, either Old or New, stand within the Norman castle on Old Sarum. Its courtyard plan would not appear, at first sight, to be one suitable to follow in the new city but, surprisingly, many of New Salisbury's houses were built in this way – indicating the generosity of its property boundaries. Life in medieval houses, great or small, revolved around the communal hall. Associated, and usually attached, to the hall was a cross-wing containing the private quarters of the family, and another containing the services – store rooms and so forth; kitchens were generally detached in rear yards. This general layout could be very varied, sometimes with the family quarters being on the floor above the services, for example. The main hall of a typical Salisbury courtyard house could be on virtually any side of that courtyard – sometimes along the street front, sometimes along one side of the courtyard and sometimes along the rear. Much depended on the owner and the value of the site for shops.

The city has more than its fair share of medieval examples and some are accessible to the public. The best place to get a real feel for the magnificence of these halls is a cinema! Although by no means the oldest example, the former hall of John Hall's house on the New Canal, in New Street Chequer, is now the foyer of the Odeon. It is actually a rather late example of an open hall, built some time in the late fifteenth century for a wealthy wool merchant who was mayor three times. Although now hemmed in on all sides, this range was originally on one flank of a courtyard. The hall itself lies behind a slightly later timber-framed frontage block, heavily restored in 1880 and completely refronted by Frederick Bath. This no doubt replaced an earlier frontage block serving the hall, and there was probably another block to the south. The

41 How many of the hundreds of cinema-goers passing through the foyer of the Odeon on New Canal realize that it is well over four hundred years old? It was the open hall of the appropriately named John Hall, a wool merchant who built this house some time after 1455. The screen is probably by Augustus Welby Pugin, who restored the building in 1834.

41 The true grandeur of John Hall's hall is in its magnificent roof, with three tiers of purlins and the ridge-piece all supported by cusped wind-braces.

hall has walls of flint and rubble, and a magnificent timber roof – six bays long with splendid trusses and wonderfully carved wind-braces supporting the three tiers of purlins and the ridge-piece. Although open halls were initially heated by fires on open hearths, this one still has its original stone fireplace. It also has the substantial remains of its medieval windows. In 1834 the hall was restored by Augustus Welby Pugin. Nearly a century later, it was again repaired, this time by W. E. Trent, architect of the Gaumont British Picture Company – now part of the Odeon group.

Bearing the sheer size of John Hall's hall in mind, it is perhaps easier to visualize the original appearance of those older examples in the city that have been altered over the years. Around the Close, where there was even more space on which to build, the traditional rural house could be built, usually with the large open hall flanked by the two cross-

19 The King's House, 65 The Close, has only been known by its present name since the late eighteenth century – simply because James I had stayed there twice. Its older name was Sherborne Place, because it belonged to the Abbots of Sherborne. To the left of the large bay window is the fifteenth-century abbot's hall, and its porch. The gables and windows are late sixteenth-century alterations, and the bay window belongs to a great parlour block added at the very end of that century. The right-hand wing is later still. It is now the Salisbury and South Wiltshire Museum.

77 The front of 29 The Close looks to be a typical piece of early nineteenth-century Regency Tudor – but the house behind the stucco probably dates to the fourteenth century. It is a fragment of a much larger building. The porch led into the screen's passage of a large hall, to the left, long since demolished. The bulk of the surviving building consists of a cross-wing attached to the hall, with grand chambers over the

wings. In fact, Elias de Dereham had laid down basic guidelines for the canons' houses in the Close at the start of the 1220s and had built his own house, Leadenhall, as an example. Only photographs of the last vestiges of this historically important house, pulled down in 1915, survive.

The finest surviving example is the Old Deanery, dating back to the thirteenth century but not generally open to the public and not easy to see. Two other medieval houses on the west side of the Close are now museums and thus are accessible. The older is the Wardrobe, 58 The Close, now a military museum. The basic stone carcass of a typical rural manor house survives. It had a central open hall flanked by two storied cross-wings that project slightly from either side to give the original house the classic 'H' plan. All this is a little difficult to see because the house has been remodelled many times in the past six centuries. That in itself makes the house a

78 The rather splendid bay window of the North Canonry was part of a major late sixteenth-century remodelling. It lit the east end of the Great Parlour on the ground floor, and the Great Chamber above. To the left was the former hall, and the driveway to the right led into the courtyard. Much medieval masonry, dating back to the thirteenth century, remains. Gilbert Scott restored the house in the nineteenth century.

79 No. 9 Queen Street was built some time after 1306 for William Russel. This is the two-storey high first floor hall at the rear of the timber-framed medieval building. The pattern of bracing is extremely unusual – perhaps unique. For many years an inserted floor within the hall hid its true character, now it is a very interesting showroom.

fascinating lesson in architectural development.

Not far away is the King's House, owned since 1979 by the Salisbury and South Wiltshire Museum. It was begun in the mid fifteenth century and the older parts are of flint rubble with tile-stiffening and stone decoration. It had the standard plan of a central open hall, with the solar wing at one end and a service wing at the other, beyond a cross-passage (or screens passage) running across the 'low' end of the hall. A porch sheltered the main door into this passage. The hall was lit by large windows and heated by a fire on the open hearth. In the roof space, remains of the louvre by which the fire's smoke eventually found its way out into the atmosphere still remains. Over the years additions and alterations have obscured the medieval features of the building, which once belonged to the Abbots of Sherborne. It was called the King's House because of visits by James I early in the seventeenth century.

68 Church House on Crane Street is another good example of a medieval hall house built where space was clearly no problem. It was built, in good quality ashlar, in the second half of the fifteenth century. To the right of the archway leading into the courtyard is the hall, restored in 1881, and just by the chimney to the right of that the windows reflect the original two storeys of the solar. The tile-hung part is an extension added when it was restored by Crickmay & Sons. Since the seventeenth century it had been the city's workhouse but was bought by the Church of England and converted into their offices.

80 These timber-framed gables, 52–4 High Street, have been famous for years because of the antiquarian book shop beneath them. The building itself, jettied on two sides, was originally three separate houses in three parallel ranges built in the fourteenth century and remarkably intact. One odd feature is the way in which the gables do not have full tie-beams. Instead, posts rising from the first floor continue into the truss itself. This may have been to do with large windows lighting the first floors, which were once open to the roof.

81 The distinctive 'St Andrew's Cross' framing of 18 St Ann's Street probably dates to the late fourteenth century. There is a tradition that it was associated with the nearby Franciscan convent but this seems unlikely. The ground floor framing has been replaced in brick.

82 'Ye House of John a Port', 8 Queen Street, actually has nothing to do with the irascible wool merchant of that name – but traditions die hard. The double-jettied three-storey timber-framed building probably dates to the mid fifteenth century and is certainly a fine specimen of its date.

83 Few people equate terraced houses with medieval towns – but they were not then uncommon. This range of seven jettied timber-framed cottages on Guilder Lane, on the east side of Swayne's Chequer, was probably built in the mid fifteenth century. Originally the rear elevation was also jettied.

84 The former Bell & Crown, now The Cloisters, on the south-east corner of Antelope Chequer, is a timber-framed building that dates back to the mid fourteenth century. The ground floor has been rebuilt in brick, and the jettied upper floor is faced with mathematical tiles.

85 The New Inn on New Street is a two-storey timber-framed building jettied to the street and probably dating to around 1500. To the right, the flint-walled gable belongs to a building possibly of fourteenth century date.

Many of the other houses around the Close, despite later facades, have medieval origins but these are so difficult to identify without venturing inside. As most are private homes, this is obviously not easy to do – but the Royal Commission's volume on the Close is well worth reading.

Back in the city, William Russel's house – 9 Queen Street – is one of the most remarkable in this remarkable city. Behind the misleading eighteenth-century front, hung with mathematical tiles, is a virtually intact timber-framed house dating to about 1314. Four bays long, the front two are three

storeys high. Until recently, so were the rear two bays, but the second floor had been inserted and was removed in 1975. The restored hall is now one of the finest showrooms in the region. In the original design the rear portion of the house consisted of a ground storey, above which was a first floor hall two storeys high and open to the apex of the roof. Although that roof is modern, the intermediate tie-beam and its amazing bracing is genuine. The support is a type of hammer-beam structure, with two tiers of curved braces forming a huge trefoiled arch over the middle of the hall – and the gaps in the spandrels were all

88 The former George Inn, in Three Swans Chequer on the corner of Winchester and Rolleston Streets, dates back to the late fifteenth century but was virtually rebuilt, in brick, in the mid seventeenth.

89 Steynings, 93 Crane Street, is a symmetrical late seventeenth-century brick house centred on a projecting porch. The easternmost bay (to the left of the photograph) has been taken over by the adjacent building and painted, damaging the original composition.

90 This lovely medium-sized town house on Payne's Hill is on the very edge of the medieval city. Built of brick with stone quoins and overhanging hipped roof, it probably dates to the end of the seventeenth century. The sundial with its 'AR' (Queen Anne) initials looks a little suspicious.

infilled with chalk rubble. In terms of architectural history this is of great importance. The earliest known hammer-beam roof is the Pilgrims' Hall in Winchester, dated by tree-ring analysis to the 1290s and much older than any others. This odd example in Salisbury is not much later. The design is also important as a good example of a first floor hall; the once jettied front part may well have contained the living quarters on the upper floors, above a shop. The hall itself was also possibly above shops, and the service wing must have been behind the hall – though that has been replaced.

Church House on Crane Street was built in the second half of the fifteenth century. The main range is faced with ashlared stone, presumably Chilmark, and lies parallel to the street. A driveway leads through to the courtyard beyond. To the right of this arched entrance was the three-bay hall, its window now restored; further right was the start of the solar portion, the

91 Mompesson House, in the north-west corner of the Close, is one of the most famous houses in Salisbury because it is owned by the National Trust. It is a good example of an early eighteenth century house, built in 1701 for Charles Mompesson whose initials are on the dated hopper heads and on the ornate wrought-iron gates. It is faced in fine quality ashlar, has a hipped roof and a good moulded eaves cornice.

private quarters of the owner, although the projecting part is part of a remodelling by Crickmay & Sons carried out in the 1880s. At the junction of these two sections on the rear, or south, wall is a splendid oriel. The house is thought to have been built for William Lightfoot, but in 1523 belonged to Thomas Coke who willed it to his delightfully named daughter – Scholastica. A hundred years later it became the city's workhouse. A new block was built along the south side of the courtyard in the eighteenth century. In 1881 the property was brought by the Church of England and much restored. They still own it – hence its modern name.

It would be wrong to think that all medieval houses were large affairs built by rich owners, and often the 'halls' were quite small rooms. Many properties were built by speculators for rent – such as the corner properties on the junction of High Street and Bridge Street – Nos 52–54 High Street, home of the

92 Even grander, though a little more gaunt, than Mompesson House, Myles Place was built on the site of a medieval canonry for William Swanton. He leased the land in 1718 and probably built the house straight away. Although like Mompesson House, it has a seven-bay ashlared facade, Myles Place is a full storey higher and also has pilasters.

93 While most of the grandest Georgian houses were being built around the Close, there were still some large houses being built in the city outside. This is The Hall, in New Street, rebuilt in its present form for William Hussey in the mid to late eighteenth century. Its unique feature is the canted first floor bay window over the entrance porch – the grandest version of the type of window seen often in Salisbury.

94 Despite appearances, this house on Castle Street was not designed as a semi-detached house, with doorways at either end on the ground floor. Instead, this was a grand town house, originally with a central door way now taken out. The building itself was probably built in the mid eighteenth century. Sadly, it has lost its original glazing bars and the blank plate glass in the sashes detracts from the overall impression.

95 Now known as Endless House (right) and Century House, this pair of late eighteenth-century town houses in Endless Street have recently been restored to something like their former glory. The cornice and overall symmetry suggests they were built as a pair – although oddly the front door in the left-hand building is off-centre. Behind the cornice is a Mansard roof. The brick bond has, as in one or two other houses of this date, mainly headers.

96 The terrace was quite popular from the eighteenth century onwards, but in a place like Salisbury could only be built where an owner had several medieval plots side by side. This plain late eighteenth-century terrace on Chipper Lane is dated 1788. The closeness of the windows to the face of the wall, and one or two odd alignments in the brick courses, may just suggest that this is faced with mathematical tiles.

97 This terrace on Trinity Street, in Marsh Chequer, was probably built towards the end of the eighteenth century and would have provided reasonable accommodation for the skilled artisans of the city. It has attics in the two-pitched 'Mansard' roof.

98 Architecturally, Trinity Hospital is perhaps the most satisfying of all the various almshouses of Salisbury. Founded in 1379, the present buildings were erected in 1702. The apparent symmetry of the composition is misleading, because the buildings are built on an oddly shaped plot of land. The frontage block is almost wedge shaped, and the rooms inside it have no right-angled corners! This view is through the entrance arch looking towards the chapel and hall across the north of the courtyard.

famous book shop. They were built in the mid-fourteenth century, and three tenements and parts of the original partitions between them survive. It would also be wrong to think that the terrace is a fairly recent innovation. There is a good example of a late fifteenth-century timber-framed terrace on Guilder Lane in Swayne's Chequer.

Towards the end of the medieval period, even the grander hall house began to go out of fashion as the hall itself did. The benefits of the widespread use of the enclosed fireplace meant rooms could be free of the need for the lofty roofs that helped get rid of the smoke of fires on the open hearths. It also meant that rooms could be lower, and more storeys fitted in to the buildings. In many cases, additional floors were simply inserted into the old halls. Communal living gave way to privacy, and general living spaces to rooms specifically designed for specific purposes – living, dining and sleeping, for example.

99 Edward Frowd 'Merch't late of this City' founded the almshouses on Bedwin Street in Parson's Chequer in 1750 for twenty-four aged people. The brick facade is fairly ordinary, but the rear, facing the gardens, has a very attractive arcade of arches – or loggia – and, on the floor above, porthole windows lighting a corridor linking the individual homes. The building was renovated and altered in 1974.

100 Hussey's Almshouses on Castle Street were founded in 1794, but the present buildings date from 1875 and are typical institutional Gothic – attractive enough in its own right, providing the houses themselves have been upgraded to modern standards for

In general terms, since the seventeenth century the overall layout of houses has changed little – except for the relatively modern requirements for separate bathrooms. The main changes have been architectural, as fashions change and the social make-up of the towns alter. By and large Salisbury has retained the basic pattern of its property boundaries and has seen little of the grand terraces so fashionable in many places. There are one or two Georgian terraces, both of middle and working class status, and several quite fine almshouses. Generally however the properties have continued to be either individually built or semi-detached. The English 'semi' is a curious phenomenon and in Salisbury as elsewhere is used in quite grand Georgian houses as well as in twentieth-century estates.

At least this ancient city has been spared the dreaded high rise, although modern maisonettes and flats have been built to the east of Exeter Street. Although dull, they at least do not

101 Brickett's Almshouses in Exeter Street were founded by Thomas Brickett for six poor widows. The present buildings, which include mock timber-framing with brick nogging, were built in 1895.

impinge on the rest of the city. It is just a shame that a little more thought could not have been given to the development and to the needs of those people who live there.

One trend in Salisbury as elsewhere has been the steady depopulation of the city centre, resulting in many properties becoming shops and offices rather than homes. In the city this process has been accelerated by the removal of houses entirely and the use of half-demolished chequers as car parks. People do still live around the fringes of the centre, thank goodness, and help retain the pleasant atmosphere of the city. Any further depopulation needs to be stopped – or reversed.

Industrial Buildings

Sleepy Salisbury is not a city readily associated with industry, yet it was an important manufacturing town until the seventeenth century. There is little evidence left of its textile industry, and nothing at all of another trade – the manufacture of high class cutlery – for which it was once renowned.

Three of the medieval bridges over the Avon that made New Salisbury an important route centre still survive more or less intact. The oldest and most important was Bishop Bingham's Ayleswade, or Harnham Bridge, built in the early 1240s of Chilmark stone. In fact there are two bridges, separated by an island in the centre of the two river channels on which the chapel of St John's still stands, heavily disguised. The northern section has three arches, the southern, six. In 1774 the bridge was widened and so the appearance of the bridge is a lot less ancient than its core. Main road traffic has now been diverted across a new bridge to the east.

The eastern arch of Crane Bridge may have some medieval elements, but the rest looks to be of seventeenth-century date, and has been widened on the downstream side at the end of the nineteenth century and again quite recently. To the east of the city, the small medieval Milford Bridge carries the former main road over the Avon's tributary, the Bourne. All the other bridges over the many water courses lacing the valley floor are fairly modern and of little interest – although Scammell's Bridge, over the river just north of the central car park at the end of Nelson Street, used to carry the railway line over Castle Street. It was moved to its present position 'without the aid of machinery' in 1898 and used as a toll bridge.

102 Ayleswade Bridge helped boost the economy of the fledgeling city of New Salisbury when it was built on the orders of Bishop Bingham in the early 1240s. The bridge diverted the main route from London to the south-west away from both Wilton and Old Sarum, and brought traffic and trade to the new city. Most of the visible masonry dates to a widening of 1774, but the original medieval bridge arches can still be seen encased in the later work.

103 Crane Bridge also has fragments of medieval masonry in it but is largely of seventeenth century date. This view shows the little altered upstream side of the bridge with a medieval arch on the left; the downstream side was widened at the end of the nineteenth century and in 1970.

The railways arrived late in Salisbury but until the end of steam working it was a major railway junction. Apart from the station itself, which has managed to keep the attractive canopies on its curving platforms, there is little left of note architecturally – although the quality and skill of the 'skew' arched bridge carrying the tracks over the Avon just south of Scammell's bridge can be appreciated.

Salisbury may have lost the once infamous water channels that ran though most of its streets, but visitors cannot fail to notice that the city enjoys an abundance of water – indeed it is one of the city's many pleasures. This water, as well as being a prime requirement of any settlement, also powered the waterwheels of mills built on the banks of the Avon or others served by mill-races – or leats – taken off the river. Two of these survive within the city, and both sites may go back to before the development of the new city.

104 Until the 1960s, Salisbury was an important railway junction and a railway enthusiast's paradise. Most of that has gone, but the station still survives as a pleasant, though not spectacular, example of Victorian railway architecture. This part of it was built in 1881.

The oldest is undoubtedly Harnham Mill, situated on the Avon and on a lovely walk which is well worth taking between the city and Harnham over the river meadows. The building is exceptionally grand for a mill, built of the chequer pattern of flint squares and ashlared Chilmark stone. The upper side walls were rebuilt in brick during the nineteenth century, but the earlier fabric is fairly complete and probably dates to the start of the sixteenth century. There is some evidence to suggest that it was built as a paper mill. In between the two World Wars, the mill was still at work, but grinding bones. It was then converted into a restaurant and guest house.

Equally attractive, though much later in date despite its detailing, is the Town Mill just off Fisherton Street. The mill site is ancient, but the present brick building is dated 1756; it was extended and the south elevation 'medievalized' with knapped flint and tall gables in 1898. More recently, it has

105 On the site of Brunel's station, sadly demolished quite recently, is the new Salisbury Train Care Depot – a clean, modern design that manages to combine utility with a little panache.

21 The walk over the water meadows to Harnham Mill is well worth the effort. The picturesque mill, with its chequer pattern walls of flint and ashlar, was probably built around 1500 and may have been a paper mill. The building to the left was built in the early nineteenth century as a warehouse attached to the mill itself.

106 The antique appearance of the Town Mill is deliberately deceptive, even though there has probably been a mill on the site for a thousand years. The present building was erected in 1756 and was given its present appearance as late as 1898. It is now part of a modern shopping

107 It is good to see that the mix of commercial and domestic buildings that was often an important part of the character of old towns and cities can still be retained. This well-restored early nineteenth-century warehouse on New Canal belonged to a shop that faced on to Silver Street. The cast-iron jib-crane is still in position by the central hoist openings.

108 The city centre bus station was built in 1939 and has been little altered in the last fifty years or so. In motor transport terms, these low neo-Georgian buildings are ancient and they are still used for their original pur pose.

been incorporated into the Maltings shopping centre and is now used for a variety of purposes – part of it being the Bishop's Mill Tavern.

Scattered around the city are the remaining buildings once associated with the infinite variety of minor industries that were needed to service the population. These include maltings, warehouses and workshops – all minor and of little obvious architectural importance, yet all integral parts of the fabric of the city.

Index

Page numbers in bold indicate illustrations.